THE RISE & RISE OF
ARIANA GRANDE

Dedicated to the Arianators, whose passion has made Ariana into the star she is today.

This book exists because of you.

First published in Great Britain in 2026
by Cassell, an imprint of
Octopus Publishing Group Ltd
Carmelite House
50 Victoria Embankment
London EC4Y 0DZ
www.octopusbooks.co.uk

An Hachette UK Company
www.hachette.co.uk

The authorized representative in the EEA is Hachette
Ireland, 8 Castlecourt Centre, Dublin 15, D15 XTP3, Ireland
(email: info@hbgi.ie)

Text copyright © Emily Zemler 2026
Design and layout copyright
© Octopus Publishing Group 2026

Distributed in the US by Hachette Book Group
1290 Avenue of the Americas, 4th and 5th Floors
New York, NY 10104

Distributed in Canada by Canadian Manda Group
664 Annette St., Toronto, Ontario, Canada M6S 2C8

Emily Zemler asserts the moral right to be
identified as the author of this work.

ISBN: 978-1-78840-639-0
eISBN: 978-1-78840-640-6

A CIP catalogue record for this book is available
from the British Library.

Printed and bound in China.

10 9 8 7 6 5 4 3 2 1

Commissioned by Stephanie Selçuk-Frank
Publisher: Trevor Davies
Senior Developmental Editor: Pauline Bache
Design: Studio Nic+Lou
Illustrator: Harriet Smeaton
Art Director: Yasia Williams
Picture Research Manager: Jennifer Veall
Assistant Production Managers: Lucy Carter
and Nic Jones

This book has not been authorised, licensed
or endorsed by Ariana Grande.

FSC
www.fsc.org
MIX
Paper | Supporting
responsible forestry
FSC® C008047

THE RISE & RISE OF
ARIANA GRANDE

The Stories Behind the Songs, Tours & Making of an Icon

Emily Zemler

CONTENTS

INTRODUCTION

It's easy to admire Ariana Grande. As a pop singer, she has an impressive vision and an even more impressive voice, both of which she channels into memorable, relatable songs that cross musical genres and balance an appreciation for nostalgia with a deft modern sensibility. As an actress, she has a rare comedic gift and a predilection for selecting projects with global appeal, from *Victorious* to *Wicked*. But, most importantly, she has been faced with immense tragedy and has always proved herself to be strong, compassionate and thoughtful in its wake. She is an avid feminist, an outspoken advocate for LGBTQ+ rights and often uses her platform to spread awareness and for the general good. Even for those who aren't self-professed fans, it would be impossible not to appreciate Ariana's influence and her impact as one of the most notable cultural icons of her generation.

Since releasing her debut album *Yours Truly* in 2013, Ariana has established herself as

BARBRA STREISAND

MADONNA

MARIAH CAREY

a modern pop diva, following in the footsteps of singers such as Barbra Streisand, Madonna, Mary J Blige and Mariah Carey. Against the odds, she seamlessly transitioned from a Nickelodeon child star into a successful musical artist, and has repeatedly shown that she can – and should – do more than one thing. Her music career spans nine No. 1 singles, seven hit albums and four world tours, and includes numerous collaborations with artists such as Nicki Minaj, Justin Bieber, Big Sean and Miley Cyrus. She's a songwriter and producer as well as a singer, and for many years now she has the been the captain of her own ship, always standing up for herself in record-label boardrooms and in the studio. Her music has been nominated for twenty Grammy Awards, two of which she's won, including for Best Pop Vocal Album for her 2018 album *Sweetener*. She's performed around the globe, hosted *Saturday Night Live* and headlined the Coachella Valley Music and Arts Festival. Her

music has become the soundtrack to people's lives, offering solace during heartbreak and encouraging joy during moments of triumph.

For almost all of her life, Ariana has bridged the gap between pop singer and actress, often pursuing both careers at the same time. After getting her start as a professional performer in the Broadway show *13* and breaking out on the children's show *Victorious*, she appeared onscreen in acclaimed films such as *Don't Look Up* and on TV shows such as *Scream Queens*. More recently, she proved that a lifelong dream is worth having. After many years of aspiring to play Glinda in the popular musical *Wicked*, Ariana embodied the character in two films, *Wicked* and its sequel *Wicked: For Good*. Her charming, disarming performance earned her an Academy Award nomination, as well as recognition at the BAFTA Awards, the Golden Globes and the SAG Awards. Although she has always expressed that music is her first love,

For almost
all of her life,

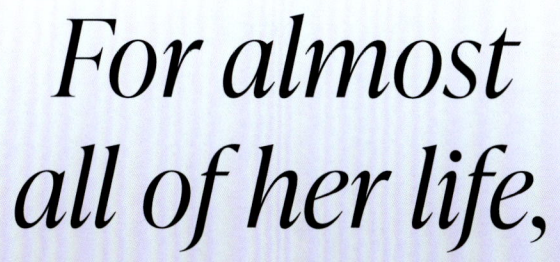

ARIANA

has bridged
the gap between
pop singer
and actress...

Ariana transitioned her career from the recording studio to the big screen with *Wicked* and the acting work that followed. In mid-2025, she acknowledged on Instagram that she was 'finding a balance, between many projects and endeavors i love, and doing it my own way.' And no matter what she does, she does it with passion and dedication.

But the journey has not always been easy for Ariana. She's dealt with public heartbreak and even more public controversy. She's been criticized for her sexuality, for her music, for her appearance and for her candidness. She's been the subject of unfair speculation about her body – something that is no one's business – and her every emotion has been splashed across tabloid front pages. In 2017, a suicide bomber attacked her concert in Manchester, killing 22 attendees and injuring hundreds more. It was devastating for Ariana, as well as for her fans and for the world. But she chose to respond to hate with kindness, and pushed the darkness out by embodying the light. Her return to music after the attack was inspiring and uplifting, and she displayed that when something bad happens, it's better to stand up than to hide away. The following year, Ariana's friend and one-time boyfriend Mac Miller died of a drug overdose, another tragedy that nearly derailed her career. But again, she persevered.

She unleashed her emotions into her music, another cathartic offering to fans, and she got back on stage and sang her heart out once more.

Going through all of this while in the spotlight can't have been easy, but Ariana has always accepted the challenges as they come and she handled these events with grace. In fact, she has always held herself to the highest standards. 'I have this idea of what I'd like to be,' she told *Vogue* in 2019. 'I can see this stronger, amazing, fearless version of myself that one day I hope to evolve into. Sometimes I try to be that for my fans before I actually am that myself.' Now in her thirties, Ariana knows she's a role model for young people – a responsibility she embraces with sincere willingness. In 2016 she told *Miss Vogue*, 'I think it's important to speak up about issues that matter and I believe we all have a responsibility to use our voices to help make a difference.' She's been steadfast in this belief and has used her own voice to encourage people to vote, to stand up for those who are bullied and to advocate for equality for women.

It's not surprising that Ariana has built such a solid fanbase over the years. She connects with her fans, known as the 'Arianators', in a genuine, interested way, often speaking to them directly on social media and at concerts, and many fans consider Ariana to be their friend. As someone who has been a fan herself and who

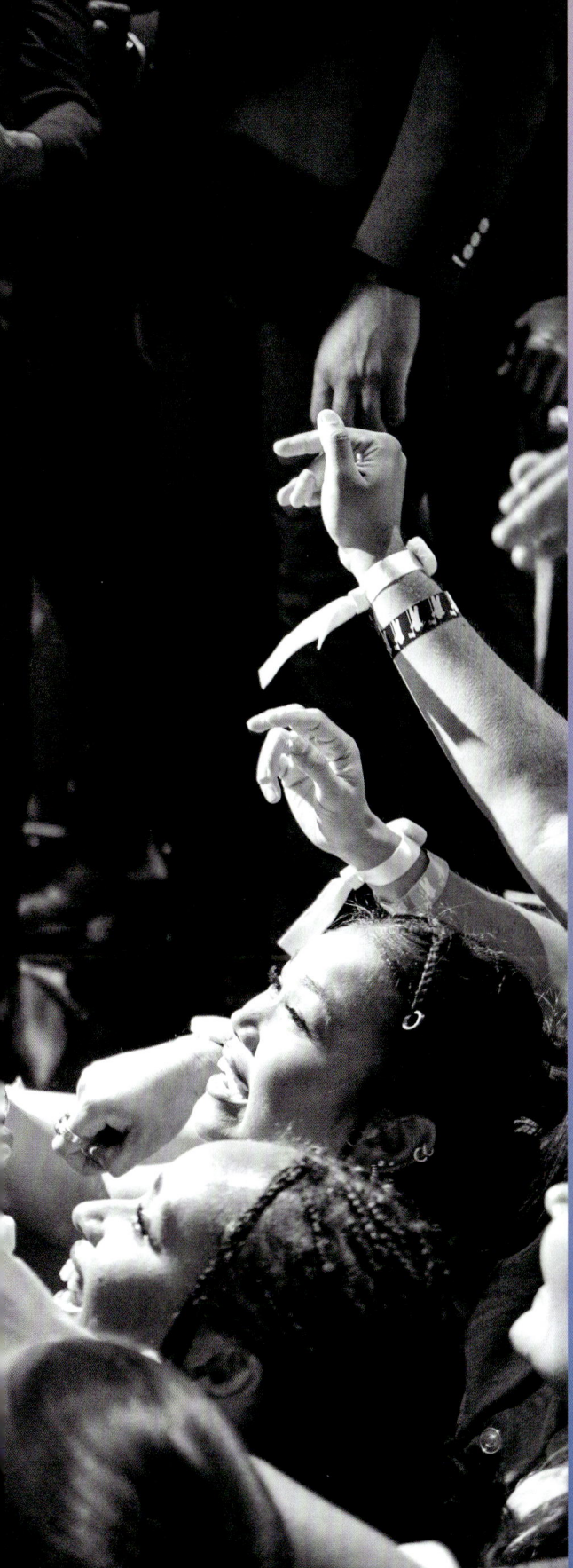

has worked with several of her own idols throughout her career, Ariana appreciates the magic of this bond. 'It's such a beautiful thing that pop music, pop culture, these films and art that we create can create a safe space for people who feel like they don't belong,' she told the *Associated Press* in 2024. 'I'm so grateful I've been able to contribute in a tiny way at all.' Whether it's at her shows or online, Ariana welcomes everyone and fosters a community of people who share her values of kindness and openness.

The Rise and Rise of Ariana Grande: The Stories Behind the Songs, Tours & Making of an Icon reflects on the many moments that have made Ariana a star. It recounts her journey from Boca Raton, Florida, to Hollywood as she pursued the dream of a career in entertainment, and reveals exactly how she became the cultural sensation she is today. Through heartache and joy, through tragedy and triumph, through hard work and sheer talent, Ariana has demonstrated her abilities to the world again and again. She's proof that we can become whoever we want to be and that we can do it in our own way. The more you learn about her story, the more you will come to appreciate her, as an artist and as a human being. 'I think it is important to stay true to who you are and pick things that you really, really love,' Ariana once said in *Miss Vogue* – a sentiment that embodies everything she has done so far. She's easy to admire, but she's even easier to enjoy.

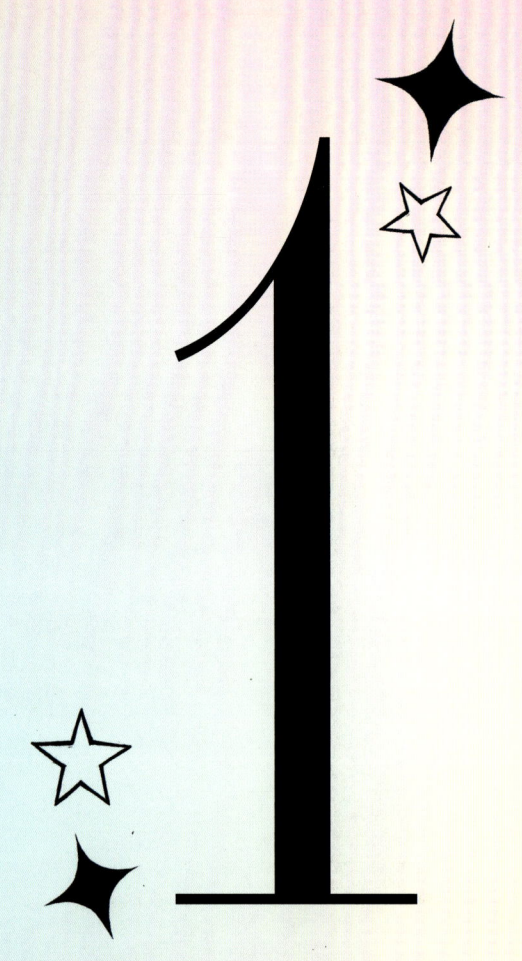

1

Just Like MAGIC

EARLY YEARS,
13 and VICTORIOUS

Ariana Grande-Butera was born on 26 June 1993 in Boca Raton, Florida. At the time, Janet Jackson's soulful pop R&B track 'That's the Way Love Goes' was enjoying an extended run at No. 1 in the US charts. It was, perhaps, a premonition for the future singer, who has always felt she possesses a gift for manifesting the future. The fact that the song was topping the charts on the week of her birth may have been a coincidence, but it seemed to herald the arrival of a promising new voice, one who would embrace the very same musical styles as Jackson in her own songs many years later. And it didn't take long for the people around Ariana to recognize her gifts for singing and songwriting, although it wasn't necessarily inevitable that Ariana would become a force to be reckoned with, both as a vocalist and as an actress. She envisioned both these careers early on and then achieved them with equal parts talent and hard work.

Ariana's parents, Joan Grande and Edward Butera, relocated to the well-off coastal city of Boca Raton from New York City shortly before her birth, a move that allowed Ariana to spend her childhood developing her talents without the external pressure of the entertainment industry.

She grew up in a gated community of Mediterranean-style homes, an idyllic setting that stood in contrast to her loud Italian family and her mom's obsession with the macabre. Joan owned a successful business selling marine-communications equipment and Edward was a graphic designer, and both worked throughout Ariana's childhood. Her older half-brother, Frankie, Joan's son with her ex, Victor Marchione, was ten years old when Ariana was born. They became lifelong best friends despite the age gap, a closeness they still share. Her grandparents, Marjorie Grande, affectionately known as Nonna, and Frank Grande, were always around, creating a boisterous, loving atmosphere and lending a

sense of support. As she once told fans on social media, her heritage is 'Italian–American, half Sicilian and half Abruzzese.'

From an early age, Ariana expressed herself in a performative way and embraced becoming different characters. She did stand-up comedy routines for her grandparents in the kitchen and donned Halloween masks throughout the year. In 2014, she described herself to *Billboard* as 'a very weird little girl' who was 'dark and deranged' and revealed that her mom once worried that she might 'grow up to be a serial killer.' 'I always wanted to have skeleton face paint on or be wearing a Freddy Krueger mask, and I would carry a hockey stick around,' Ariana explained. 'I was like a mini-Helena Bonham Carter. For my fifth birthday party we had a *Jaws* theme and all my friends left crying.'

It was Joan, a self-described goth who attended the artistically inclined Barnard College in New York, who emboldened Ariana to be so expressive. It was also Joan who kept music perpetually blaring through the house and in the car, encouraging Ariana and Frankie to sing along. Once, when Ariana was three and a half years old, the family was in the car

listening to NSYNC as Joan drove. Ariana hit JC Chasez's high notes with perfect pitch, another glimmer of her possible future. Joan immediately pulled the car over and asked, 'Ariana, was that you?' And, of course, it was. Songs by renowned divas such as Whitney Houston, Madonna, Mariah Carey and Celine Dion were on heavy rotation, as were classic artists such as Frank Sinatra and Dean Martin. Ariana loved old musicals starring Judy Garland, whom she admired. 'I would stand in front of the TV and mimic her body movements,' she told *Vogue* in 2019. 'I was always fascinated. She carried herself in a way that was so protected and soft and Judy.'

Frankie, too, inspired Ariana. He was a performer himself, with a love for musical theatre and dancing. The family regularly visited New York City to see the current Broadway shows, and Ariana cultivated an early adoration for the genre. 'Once Frankie got into acting in musical theatre and dancing, I was like, "Okay, I guess that's the cool thing now, so let's investigate and watch old musicals,"' Ariana told *The Daily Telegraph* in 2014. Frankie recognized Ariana's talent, although he never imagined

PERFORMING IN TIMES SQUARE WITH THE CAST OF *13*   WITH ELIZABETH EGAN GILLIES, MARK INDELICATO AND MIRANDA COSGROVE

how far she would go. 'I'm so proud of her because she's someone who at a very young age knew what she wanted to do, pursued it, and succeeded to an extent none of us could have foreseen,' he told *Attitude* in 2016. 'And she did that herself; she's not the product of any sort of machine.'

Like those around her, Ariana understood her artistic calling in an unusually perceptive way. When she was four years old, she called the information line 411 and asked to be connected with Universal Studios in Orlando, Florida. 'By some miracle I got through,' she recounted on *The Tonight Show* in 2021. She asked the person who answered if she could join the cast of one of Nickelodeon's popular shows, either *All That* or *The Amanda Show* – she didn't care which. This fearlessness led to other memorable moments throughout her childhood, for example, when she belted out the *Titanic* theme song 'My Heart Will Go On' at karaoke on a cruise ship. By happenstance,

singer Gloria Estefan and her family were also onboard and witnessed the precocious performance. Estefan was so impressed she invited Ariana over to say hello. She told her, 'You keep singing. I never would have done that at your age. You've got a gift. Keep going.' The elder singer's message underscored something Ariana already knew about herself: there was only one path forward. 'When I was six years old, I just kind of decided that's what I'm going to do with my life, period,' she told *Billboard* in 2018. 'I manifested it. I knew I would. There was never really a doubt in my mind.'

When Ariana was eight years old, her parents got divorced. It was a challenging hurdle in an otherwise idyllic upbringing. The couple's relationship became strained in the years that followed, although on the *Zach Sang Show* in 2024 the singer acknowledged that she understood in hindsight why they had split up. 'Growing up, you want what you don't have,' she

'I manifested it.
I knew I would.
There was
never really a
DOUBT
in my mind.'

reflected. She felt that her parents 'got divorced for all the right reasons,' and worried that craving a 'happily ever after' could become problematic. 'So you ignore all these issues and you cling on to that fairytale,' she added. 'You self-abandon. And I think my mom is a fierce example of not doing that.' The dissolution of her parents' marriage had a substantial impact on Ariana. It's not hard to imagine that's why she began to write and sing about relationships later in her career, a thematic undercurrent that has always pervaded her work – her ongoing examination of what brings two people together and what can tear them apart may have been rooted in her imagination since long before she was a pop star. But despite the pain of the divorce, Ariana never lost her faith in love.

Around the same time that her parents split up, Ariana began to pursue acting and singing in earnest. She flawlessly performed 'The Star-Spangled Banner' at ice-hockey team the Florida Panthers' home game against the Chicago Blackhawks on 16 January 2002. That same year, she auditioned for a production of the musical *Annie* at the Boca Raton community theatre, Little Palm Family Theatre, and was cast in the title role. 'I was very sick,' she recalled to *The Hollywood Reporter* of the audition with the community theatre. 'I had bronchitis, but I really wanted to go.' Because parents weren't allowed to attend the rehearsals, Joan also auditioned and got two roles, an apple seller and one of Daddy Warbucks' housekeepers, subjecting herself to the play purely so she could support Ariana's dream. From the start, acting and singing felt like a welcome refuge for Ariana, who could feel herself discovering the right path. 'I remember

WITH MOTHER JOAN AND HALF-BROTHER FRANKIE

'I loved playing a

CHARACTER

as it was sort of just taking a vacation from myself.'

saying, "Mommy, I never want this to end,"' Ariana told *The Daily Telegraph*. 'I loved playing a character as it was sort of just taking a vacation from myself.'

In 2003, the Little Palm Family Theatre staged a production of *The Wizard of Oz* – a story that would come to define Ariana's life and career – with Ariana as Dorothy Gale. It was a full-circle moment for her, as someone who had studied Garland intensely, particularly when Ariana took to the stage to sing 'Over the Rainbow.' Soon after, when Ariana was ten years old, she and Joan founded the children's theatre troupe Kids Who Care, which performed around Boca Raton at charity events. Ariana's future Broadway co-star Aaron Simon Gross was a fellow member. It was clear that Ariana had a strong work ethic and unflagging drive. She was always eager to be part of every theatre production, regardless of her role. 'I just wanted to do every single show,' she told *Billboard*. 'However many there were in a year, I was in every one, whether I was a chorus girl or the lead or doing the lighting.'

By 14 years old, Ariana began to take things more seriously. During her freshman year at private high school North Broward Preparatory School, Ariana attended an open audition for the Broadway production of *13*. Featuring music and lyrics by Jason Robert Brown and a book adaptation by Dan Elish and Robert Horn, this was the first Broadway musical to star an entire cast of teenagers. It had premiered in Los Angeles in 2007, but was recast before moving to Chester, Connecticut, in the summer of 2008, and then onward to Broadway's Bernard B Jacobs Theatre that September. Ariana sang a Mariah Carey song for her audition and was given the role of Charlotte, marking her professional acting debut. 'She opened her mouth and we said, "We have cast her,"' Brown told *Grammy.com* in 2022. 'She was always an extraordinarily talented creature.'

After several weeks of previews, *13* opened on Broadway on 5 October 2008. 'There really aren't words to describe how incredible this feeling is,' Grande told *Broadway.com* on opening night. 'Not only to be making your Broadway debut at such a young age, but this whole cast is like a family and we're all together and we have each other's backs. This is so incredible.' Ariana appeared alongside actress and singer Elizabeth Gillies, who played Lucy,

WITH DANIELLA MONET, MATT BENNETT AND VICTORIA JUSTICE

and the pair, who became lifelong friends, eventually starred on Nickelodeon together. The show ran for 105 performances and closed on 4 January 2009. It represented exactly where Ariana wanted to be at the time. 'I really thought I'd be a Broadway girl forever,' Grande told *The Hollywood Reporter* in 2024. 'I mean, that was the dream: I'd be in New York City doing eight shows a week, and then maybe on the side I'd be able to do music, and some people would want to hear it.'

But Ariana soon left the lights of Broadway behind. Only weeks after the musical concluded, she booked her next gig on Nickelodeon children's series *Victorious*, a sitcom created by Dan Schneider. It was the materialization of her early dream to appear on one of the American television network's shows. Ariana initially auditioned for *Victorious* in New York City while *13* was still on Broadway. She auditioned alongside Gillies, and the pair were later flown out to Los Angeles for callbacks. It was Ariana's first time in the Californian city. In 2022, she told Kelly Clarkson on *The Kelly Clarkson Show* that she remembered being 'so nervous, but so excited.' Joan was supportive, as usual. She asked Ariana if she thought she could 'really do this' and the answer was a confident 'yes.' But a nerve-wracking amount of time passed between the callback and more auditions. Joan committed to a short-term lease apartment in Los Angeles despite Ariana having not yet received official word from the studio. She was eventually cast as Cat Valentine, a sweet,

emotional student at the fictional performing-arts school Hollywood Arts High School.

Although Ariana had imagined herself on Broadway, she later explained that she went for *Victorious* because it felt like the logical next step in her career. 'I never really saw myself as an actress, but when I started talking about wanting to make R&B music at 14, they were like, "What the fuck would you sing about? This is never going to work. You should audition for some TV shows and build yourself a platform and get yourself out there, because you're funny and cute and you should do that until you're old enough to make the music you want to make,"' Ariana told *Vogue*. 'So I did that. I booked that TV show, and then I was like, "OK, now can I make music?"' But for the moment, the music industry wasn't

ready for Ariana. Instead, she focused on embodying Cat, a formative character with whom she would forever be associated.

Nickelodeon brought the cast of *Victorious* out to Los Angeles in the fall of 2009 to begin production. Along with lead actress Victoria Justice and Gillies, Ariana was joined by Leon Thomas III, Matt Bennett, Avan Jogia and Daniella Monet. The show was filmed at the Nickelodeon studios on Sunset in Hollywood and primarily used sets rather than real locations, including for the high school's interiors. The actors bonded quickly. 'Ariana was the only person in the cast I knew beforehand, but it only took about a day for us all to really hit it off,' Gillies told *Seventeen*. 'I knew after the first day on set that our cast was going to be

like a family and luckily I was right. We all get along really great.' Ariana later confirmed to the magazine, 'My years filming *Victorious* were some of the happiest of my life and that cast is family to me.'

To play Cat, Ariana dyed her hair a vibrant red. 'It took a second for me to really, really, really get used to it,' Ariana told *ClevverTV.com*. 'But I'm not opposed to it and I think it's fun.' Nickelodeon asked Ariana to make the change from her natural brunette locks because they wanted Cat to stand out, but also because the character was 'kind of zany and out there,' as Ariana explained. The colour would become perpetually associated with Cat. 'It's kind of like the red was Cat, and that was very much a character, and it was very much a portion of my life that I love and I am so grateful for,' she reflected on the *Zach Sang Show* in 2020. She added that it was not a true representation of her, but something she did for the role. 'I think fondly of that,' she noted of the colour. 'But again, it is not me.'

Victorious premiered on 27 March 2010 and ran for four seasons. Ariana's experience on the show was complicated. Being a child star was taxing and there was drama behind the scenes,

including alleged misconduct by Schneider. The accusations against the showrunner were brought to light in 2024 in the Investigation Discovery series *Quiet on Set: The Dark Side of Kids TV*. Although many of the actors from Schneider's shows did appear in the documentary, Ariana did not, and nor did she directly address the allegations. But Gillies confirmed in an interview with *Variety* that they watched the series together. 'I certainly re-evaluated my experience with Ariana over FaceTime,' Gillies said of their time on *Victorious*. 'We watched it together, and then we got together later that week or the next week, and we sort of broke the whole thing down and talked about it, and reprocessed everything together. There was a lot to go through.' Gillies added that she felt lucky to have had such a close relationship with the cast, including Ariana, because they were all able to lean on and check in with each other.

Speaking on the *Podcrushed* podcast after the documentary series aired, Ariana affirmed that she had been 'reprocessing' her relationship with the show. She acknowledged that one of the 'beautiful things' to come from her time on *Victorious* was that she and Gillies

WITH LEON THOMAS III, APOLO ANTON OHNO AND ELIZABETH GILLIES

'got to fall in love with these characters that we created, and learn what it feels like to be so in a character that you can't separate yourself from it.' She said the reflection pushed her to call for the environments on kids' shows to be 'made safer' in general. She also expressed concern about some of the content on *Victorious*. 'I think that was something that we were convinced was the cool thing about us – is that we pushed the envelope with our humour,' she said. 'I think it just all happened so quickly and now looking back on some of the clips I'm like, "Damn, really?"'

When it premiered, *Victorious* wasn't particularly controversial; in fact, it had a substantial pop-culture impact. The show was immediately beloved by fans, particularly young ones. It was ultimately nominated for four Emmys, and twice won Favorite TV Show at the Nickelodeon Kids' Choice Awards. The series and its position in the pop-culture zeitgeist launched Ariana into the public

sphere, a jarring experience that left her somewhat unsettled. 'I was adjusting to these new things – red carpets, and people wanting pictures with me, and people taking pictures of me when I didn't know they were being taken,' she told *The Daily Telegraph*. She enjoyed performing, she said, but along with the attention came a lot of 'weird superficial nonsense' to which she was unaccustomed.

Ariana experienced her first red carpet at the premiere of Wes Anderson's film *Fantastic Mr. Fox* in 2009. It taught her early on how to make fashion choices for public events. 'I had my red hair and my little green mini dress and I remember I felt really cute,' she recalled to *The Hollywood Reporter*. She also began wearing her hair in a ponytail around that time, a style that has become iconic for the singer. Ariana adopted the look in part because her real hair had broken off after dying it for *Victorious*, but also as part of her public persona. 'The hair for me is such a guard, character-facade type thing,

WITH LISA NICOLE WILKERSON, JEN BENDER AND ALICE RIPLEY

and it's had its own evolution, but it has always been this kind of costume piece,' she said on the *Zach Sang Show*. She later told *Byrdie.com* that her signature look was like 'true love.' 'It brings me so much joy, honestly,' she said. 'Every time I put my hair up, it's like a surprise. Like, I forget how much I love it, and then I tie it back and I'm like, "I love this look! Ooh, girl!" Every time I tie it up is like the first time.'

Because *Victorious* was a series about students at a performing-arts high school, it did offer Ariana a platform to perform music, although it was not her own. Nickelodeon released three soundtracks for the show, including *Victorious: Music from the Hit TV Show* in 2011 and *Victorious 3.0: Even More Music From the Hit TV Show* in 2012. Ariana had the opportunity to collaborate with Gillies on 'Give It Up', which initially appeared on the show in 2010 as part of the one-hour special episode 'Freak the Freak Out'. The pop song was officially released the following year and

marked the musical debut for both actresses. Ariana followed it with 'L.A. Boyz', a duet with Victoria Justice. The bubblegum-pop track featured a hooky chorus and a youthful ebullience, with Ariana taking on the soaring harmonies. Still, she wanted to make her own music, not simply perform what was asked of her on the show.

Ariana soon realized that if she wanted to sing outside of *Victorious* she would have to make it happen for herself. She launched a YouTube channel in 2007 under the name 'osnapitzari', a stylization of 'Oh snap, it's Ari.' She began uploading vlogs, funny videos and cover songs. The first song she ever wrote and recorded was called 'Let It Rain.' The buoyant song, inspired by Natasha Bedingfield and Mary J Blige, had simple but thoughtful lyrics about accepting whatever comes your way. Ariana wrote it when she was only 12 years old and self-recorded it the following year, eventually posting it on her YouTube. 'I just

loved it,' she said of the track during an appearance on the podcast *Podcrushed*. 'I just wanted to create.' One of Ariana's earliest covers was India Arie's 'There's Hope', performed using a loop pedal machine to create rich vocal layers. Her efforts spanned multiple genres, often focusing on artists with similarly impressive range or on emotionally evocative songs. It was her 2012 version of Justin Bieber's 'Die in Your Arms' that caught the attention of manager Scooter Braun, who signed her shortly after. 'She's the real deal,' Braun told *Complex* in 2013. 'I don't think she needs to worry about anything other than being who she is.'

In order for Ariana to move forward as a singer, she would need to find the time to focus on songwriting – something that was not easy to do while also filming *Victorious*. But as much as she knew what she wanted to do, doubts lingered. Not about herself, but about how the industry would treat her if she pursued acting and music simultaneously. 'I didn't ever think that I would be seen as a singer,' she admitted to *The Hollywood Reporter* in 2025. 'I hoped. I hoped that people would let me do both or that I would be able to do both with my life.' At the time, it seemed unfathomable. However, while success in the entertainment industry requires big dreams and hard work; Ariana had both. At only 17 years old, she was ready to step into her destiny to become a pop singer.

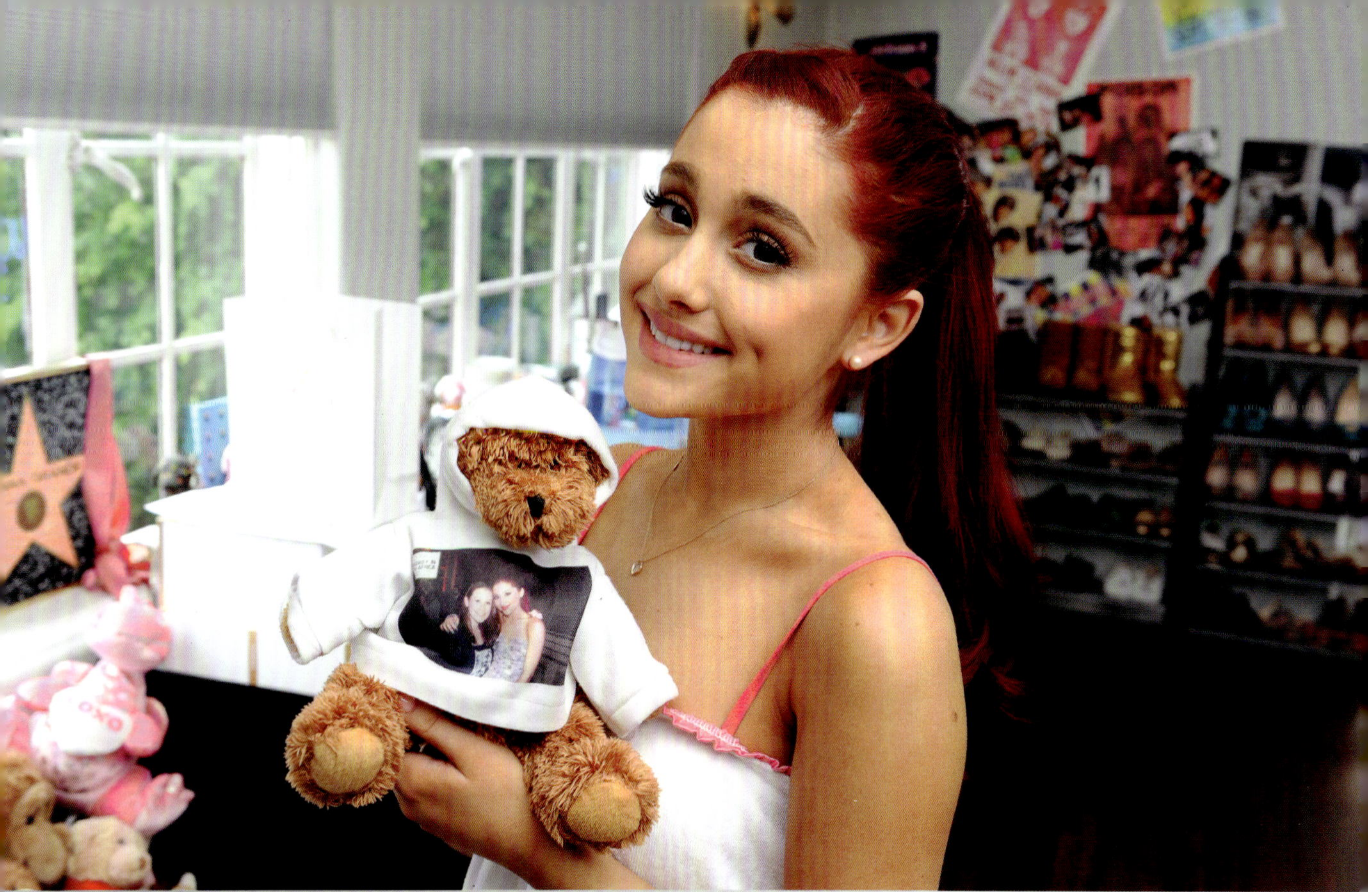

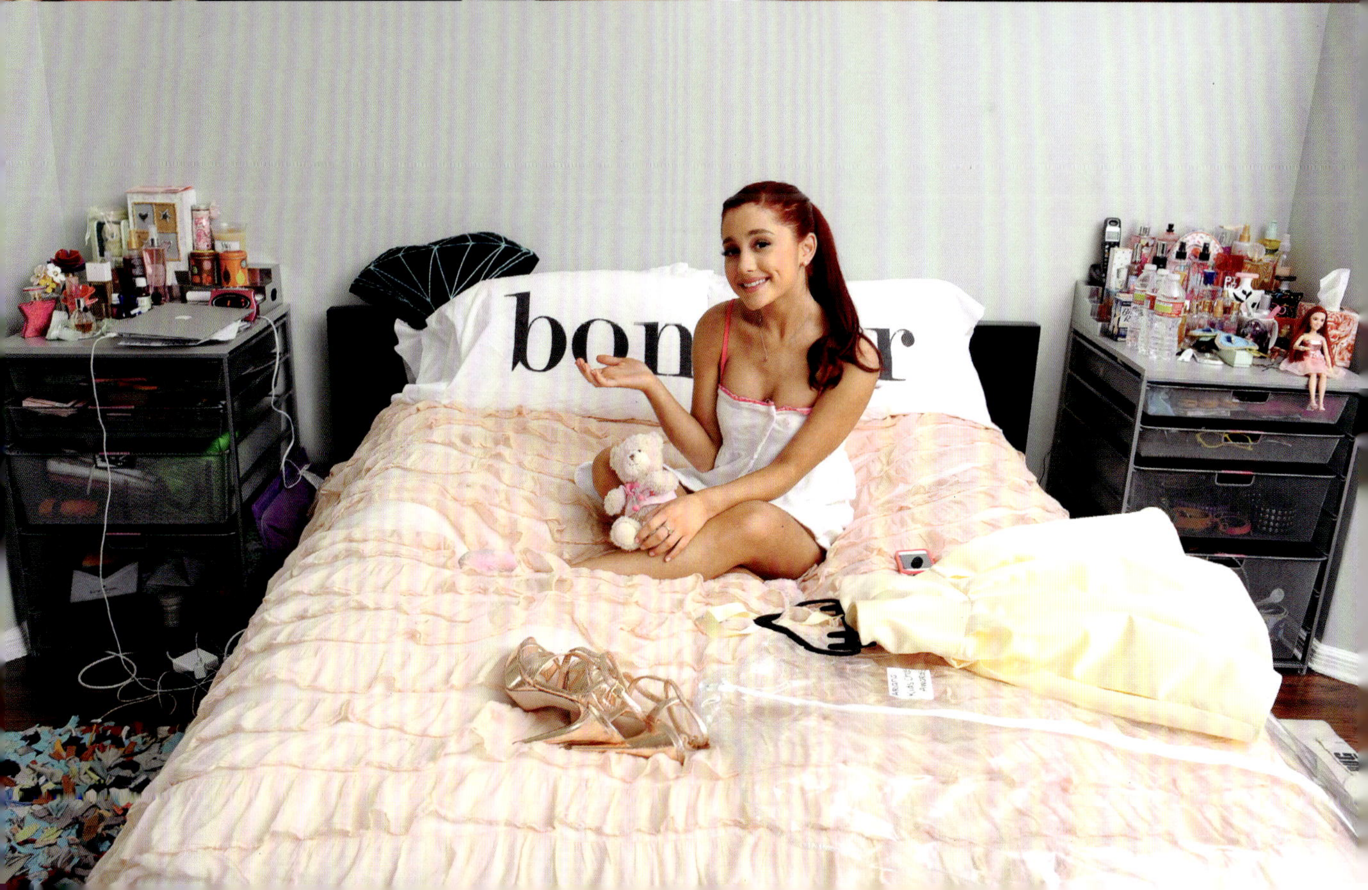

2

Break FREE

YOURS TRULY, MY EVERYTHING and ACCLAIM

As an overachiever, Ariana was undeterred by the challenge of pursuing dual careers and began writing and recording her debut album *Yours Truly* in 2010 while still in production on *Victorious*. Creating the songs became an obsession for the singer, who told *ELLE* in 2013 that she preferred creating music to acting. 'If I could, I would not do anything else,' Ariana admitted. 'I'd just be in the studio for my whole life.' She said she would never go to parties or events, but would be in the studio the whole time. 'I don't even care,' she added. 'Nobody has to know what I look like. I just want to make music.' Initially, Ariana wrote songs in her bedroom using the recording software GarageBand, a process she described as 'very Imogen Heap-inspired.' But after she

signed with her record label, Republic Records, Ariana transitioned to collaborating with top-tier producers in big recording studios.

By the time her record-label deal was announced in August of 2011, Ariana had already finished more than 20 songs. Some tracks, such as 'Honeymoon Avenue' and 'Tattooed Heart', were re-recorded and rearranged in the studio to ensure a sonic continuity on the album. 'It was a complete transformation – at least for "Honeymoon Avenue",' Ariana recalled to *ELLE*. 'It started off as an upbeat, rooftop-down summer song, and it turned out being almost six minutes long. It's this gorgeous, mid-tempo sad song.' She spent the coming months in and out of the studio with producers including Kenneth 'Babyface' Edmonds, Matt Squire, Harmony Samuels,

PROMOTING 'PUT YOUR HEARTS UP' IN DECEMBER 2011

Tommy Brown and The Rascals. She embraced a range of influences and genres, from pop to R&B to doo-wop, often showcasing a nostalgic flair for the musical styles of decades past.

In December of 2011, Ariana released 'Put Your Hearts Up', an upbeat pop single that was targeted at her young fanbase from *Victorious*. The song, written with Matt Squire, Linda Perry and Martin Johnson, may have been a hit with that audience, but didn't properly tease Ariana's impending album. It also didn't reflect where she ultimately wanted her music to go. 'It was a

learning experience for sure,' she later said during an interview on the *Kidd Kraddick Morning Show*. 'Sonically, it's just not my vibe.' While she thought it would have been a great hit song for somebody else, it wasn't what she wanted to sing. 'It's a bubblegum pop record, for sure, and I like to sing stuff that's a little more soulful,' she added. 'I love pop music, I'm a huge pop music fan, but I just didn't think that that record was right for me.' As Ariana began to finalize the track list for *Yours Truly*, 'Put Your Hearts Up' didn't make the cut. Instead, she

'I'm finally at
an age where
I can do the

MUSIC

that I grew
up loving...'

leaned more heavily on her love of Motown and 50s and 60s soul music, as well as 90s pop, preferring a retro style to a current one.

Ariana eventually declared her musical intentions on 26 March 2013 when she debuted 'The Way', her album's flagship single and a collaboration with up-and-coming rapper Mac Miller. *Victorious* had come to an official end only a month before, signalling a new chapter in the singer's career. She was already in the middle of shooting the show's spin-off series *Sam & Cat*, which was set to premiere over the summer, but her focus was clearly on new music. 'The Way' was co-written by Ariana with Amber Streeter, Al Sherrod Lambert, Jordin Sparks, Brenda Russell and Samuels, and sampled Big Pun's 1998 song 'Still Not a Player'. It came out of a writing session with Samuels, who had initially recorded a demo of the track with Sparks on vocals. After hearing the demo, Ariana recorded a new version of the song and then approached Miller, her good friend, with the idea for him to guest on the track.

When Ariana played the song for the rapper, he replied, 'Sounds like a hit to me.' She joined him in the studio as he crafted his verses, and told *Billboard* that she would bake cookies in the kitchen upstairs while he recorded his parts. 'Every time I took a break I came into the studio to bring him a new batch of cookies and something else amazing had been written,' she said. She added that the song aptly reflected her present approach to songwriting and her focus on doing music that she was passionate about. 'I'm finally at an age where I can do the music that I grew up loving, which was urban pop, 90s music. I grew up listening to the divas, so I'm very happy to finally do urban pop.'

The flirtatious single was a notably mature evolution for Ariana, who was 19 when it came out. The energetic music video, which also featured Miller, was similarly coy, spotlighting an amorous back and forth between the two singers. The pair shot the video with director Jones Crow and didn't tell Ariana's record label in advance that they were going to make it. The singer described creating it on 'no budget' when answering fan questions on TikTok for the tenth anniversary of her debut album *Yours Truly*. '[We] made it ourselves, and we said, "Listen, we have a camera, we have a projector, we have music, we have balloons, we got dancers,"' she said. 'We didn't have any budget or anything, we just made it. [We] showed it to the label, because they brought it up to me. They were like, "We need to shoot a music video," and I was like, "We already did it."'

The music video memorably featured a kiss between Ariana and Miller, who didn't officially start dating until several years later, in 2016. Many fans picked up on the tension between the pair, which Ariana later admitted was always present. 'We have loved and adored and respected each other since the beginning, since before we even met, just because we were fans of each other's talent,' she told *Cosmopolitan* in 2017. 'We weren't ready at all, though, to be together. It's just timing. We both needed to experience some things, but the love has been there the whole time.' There had been times over the years when Miller would call her and, if she seemed stressed or overwhelmed, he would let Ariana's mother know. 'There were also times when he was really broken and sad – this was years ago – and I would come take

WITH MAC MILLER

MAC MILLER

AALIYAH

care of him, because we love each other as best friends first and foremost,' she noted.

'The Way' drew apt comparisons to Mariah Carey for its soulful, high-energy vocals, which *Rolling Stone* described as verging on 'ecstatic.' Ariana sounded free to be herself on the track, revelling in a newfound sense of liberation. Although it was light-hearted, summer-ready fare, it contained enough heft to signal that Ariana was serious about her musical career. 'The Way' emphasized that she could do more than star on Nickelodeon shows for kids and cemented her intention: to make real music as a real singer. In an interview for *Hard Knock TV*, Miller acknowledged that it would be easy to write Ariana off as an actress-turned-singer. 'But she could really do this,' he said. 'I think she will, so it's awesome and I'm glad I was part of one of the first things she did.' The single was an immediate success and debuted at No. 10

on the *Billboard* Hot 100 chart. It ultimately spent 26 weeks on the chart, and in 2014 was certified triple platinum by the Recording Industry Association of America, selling more than 3 million copies in the US.

In May 2013, Ariana showcased 'The Way' at KIIS-FM's Wango Tango concert in Los Angeles, followed by a televised performance on *The Ellen DeGeneres Show*. The following month, she and Miller performed it together on *Late Night with Jimmy Fallon*. In July, Ariana released the album's second single, 'Baby I,' a pop R&B song about not being able to voice your feelings for someone you love. It was Miller who suggested Ariana release 'Baby I' after the success of 'The Way.' 'That's honestly the only reason why it was the second single,' Ariana admitted to *Complex*. She'd been sceptical about it, but loved the song. 'It feels a lot like *Dreamgirls* to me,' she said. 'It's so

DESTINY'S CHILD

BIG SEAN

glamorous [...]I feel like it shows off my musicality more than "The Way" did – vocally and just the song itself is such a statement and that's what I love about it. "Baby I" is special in the way it's just musical.'

'Baby I' acted as a companion piece to 'The Way.' Both were sophisticated and grown-up, and reflected Ariana's musical predilections. It paid homage to 90s pop, evoking artists such as Aaliyah and Destiny's Child, both of whom Ariana cited as inspirations. The song detailed having a crush but being unable to express the emotion fully – a relatable theme for many of her listeners. Rather than approach the subject in a pessimistic way, she imbued the lyrics with a sense of levity and charm. 'I love what it says,' Ariana told *MTV News*. 'I love it's about loving somebody so much that you just don't know what to say. I think that's really cute. I laughed the first time I heard the lyrics.' The song had

personal resonance because she found it difficult to express herself with other people, especially at the beginning of a crush or relationship. 'I'm so awkward and so flustered in that way. I'm always so nervous to express myself that I feel like it's a very me song in that way.'

Only a few weeks after dropping 'Baby I', Ariana shared another single, 'Right There', which featured vocals from her pal Big Sean. The buoyant song saw Ariana and Big Sean trading verses, each acknowledging that they would always be there for their significant other. It nodded to Ariana's still-innocent nature, albeit with a sly wink, and it underscored her love of 90s R&B. The single again garnered comparisons to Carey, which Ariana told *Rolling Stone* was a 'blessing' rather than something that pigeonholed her work. 'It's a massive compliment,' Ariana said.

'She's the greatest singer in the world, like literally, the *Guinness Book of World Records*. It's an incredible compliment, but it doesn't worry me because when you listen to my album as a whole, you get to know me.' A *Romeo & Juliet*-inspired music video for 'Right There' arrived in October, starring actor Patrick Schwarzenegger and Ariana's longtime friend Elizabeth Gillies, as well as Big Sean himself. Like the single, the video offered an early glimpse into Ariana's preference for songs about romantic relationships, a fascination that became a foundation of her musical career.

Although 'Right There' marked the third and final pre-release single for *Yours Truly*, Ariana shared an additional song before the album was released on 30 August 2013. A week before, she unveiled 'Almost Is Never Enough', which featured The Wanted singer Nathan Sykes, who Ariana was dating at the time. It was included on the soundtrack of the fantasy film *The Mortal Instruments: City of Bones*, and showcased a slower, more soulful side of the singer. The anthemic ballad was deeply emotional, highlighting Ariana's ability to let her voice carry a song without the distraction of ornate pop production. It also set the stage for the album itself, a collection of vocal-driven tracks that reminded fans of Ariana's singular talent, as well

as her love of diverse musical genres. *The New York Times* called *Yours Truly* a 'surprisingly strong album', writing, 'She has a lithe voice and is capable of real power, though she doles it out carefully. Like that other child TV star turned pop comer Miley Cyrus, Ms. Grande is twenty, but her slide into maturity isn't moving at Ms. Cyrus's warp speed. Ms. Grande's version of adulthood is about expertise, not transgression.'

Yours Truly was a declaration of intention for Ariana. It was her way of sharing herself, rather than one of her fictional acting characters, with the world. Around the time of the album's release, she told *Complex* that she didn't feel the music was a reintroduction because fans didn't actually know her yet. 'They know me as Cat, so I think of it as an introduction to Ariana,' she said. 'It's not something I think about, "How can I show the world I'm grown up? I'm sexy or more mature." I don't feel comfortable flaunting my body that much yet. I don't need to do that to show I'm grown up. I don't want people to talk about my choices or how little I'm wearing. I just want the conversation to be about the music and what I'm creating.'

Ahead of the album's release, Ariana joined Justin Bieber for three shows on his Believe Tour in August 2013 and also embarked on her

own mini-tour, The Listening Sessions. Although Ariana had experience performing night after night on Broadway, she hadn't previously toured as a musical artist. She took the preparation very seriously and rehearsed extensively. She learned to work with in-ear monitors, used by singers onstage to hear their backing music, and took as much vocal rest as possible. Ariana herself was responsible for determining how best to showcase her songs live. 'I'm helping arrange everything because I'm incredibly anal,' she told *MTV News*. 'So I'm helping arrange the parts for the backup singers, the horns, the violins, the band, and everything.' She described her approach to the shows as 'very hands-on.'

Although the shows were a success, Ariana didn't have time in her *Sam & Cat* production schedule for a full tour. The Nickelodeon show had premiered in June to mixed reviews and had since been airing weekly. After a summer hiatus, filming resumed on the second half of the series' first season. Despite her lack of free time, Ariana embraced the momentum of *Yours Truly* the best that she could. She won New Artist of the Year at the American Music Awards and released a four-song holiday EP, *Christmas Kisses*, in December. And, as busy as she was, Ariana was already hard at work on her second album, *My Everything*.

Rather than allowing the songs on *Yours Truly* to linger, Ariana began writing and recording new music almost immediately after the album dropped. 'I'm a workaholic, and a perfectionist,' she explained to *Billboard*. 'It was a very exciting thing for me to all of a sudden have this new mission, to make something as special as *Yours Truly*, and to put my time and effort into something new and something I want to make just as good, if not better.' In

"PROBLEM"

truly represents the feeling of being absolutely terrified to reapproach a relationship that's gone sour – but you want to more than anything.'

April 2014, less than a year after the release of *Yours Truly*, Ariana debuted 'Problem', the first single off her sophomore LP. The upbeat R&B pop number was a collaboration with Australian rapper Iggy Azalea, who Ariana met at Katy Perry's MTV EMA's afterparty in 2013. It was co-written by Max Martin and Savan Kotecha. Kotecha revealed that the single's memorable hook was inspired by something he read in *Cosmopolitan* magazine. 'I keep a list of titles and phrases in my phone that I hear or read from a movie or a magazine,' the writer and producer told *Mic*. 'And then, a lot of the times, I build a melody around them.'

According to Ariana, 'Problem' was about moving on from someone toxic. Although she never specifically referenced an ex of her own, she did admit that the lyrics resonated with her personally. '"Problem" truly represents the feeling of being absolutely terrified to re-

approach a relationship that's gone sour – but you want to more than anything,' she told *Billboard*. 'In the song, it ends on a sappy, negative note, but in [real] life, we're hoping it's going to end on a positive one. I feel like it's all very honest and human.' It was catchy, too, featuring a 90s-inspired saxophone loop and a thumping beat. The song was modern, but with throwback elements that felt revelatory to critics and fans alike. *MTV* called it 'the freshest pop song of the moment' and *Pitchfork* named it 'Best New Track', proclaiming that the single 'bears all the hallmarks of a future smash'. And it was a massive hit. 'Problem' debuted at No. 3 on the *Billboard* Hot 100 chart, marking Ariana's second single to debut in the Top 10 after 'The Way'. The song's colourful, mod-inspired music video, which featured an appearance by Kaz James, arrived in May and surpassed 100

WITH KATY PERRY

WITH IGGY AZALEA

million views in only two months. It later won the MTV VMA for Best Pop Video.

Ariana went on a promotional blitz for 'Problem'. In April, she performed the single live at the 2014 Radio Disney Music Awards. In May, she showcased the track at the 2014 iHeartRadio Music Awards and on *The Ellen DeGeneres Show*. She and Azalea shared the stage at KIIS-FM 102.7's annual Wango Tango concert, performing the song for the first time live together, and again at the 2014 *Billboard* Music Awards. It was a ubiquitous track, taking over TV and radio as the summer arrived. Its edgy, bad-girl vibe showcased an evolution for Ariana, who had explicitly said she wanted to try something different on her second album.

The buzz around the single led to even more hype for Ariana's follow-up to *Yours Truly*. 'Ariana Grande's 2013 debut album *Yours Truly* was a frustrating one – she clearly has the chops to make waves in the pop world, but it was deeply unclear who she really was as an artist,' *Entertainment Weekly* wrote. 'Perhaps she's doing some soul-searching, because her new single "Problem", which just dropped today, is a dramatic reinvention.'

As Ariana was plotting the release of *My Everything*, *Sam & Cat* was reaching the end of its first season. The cast had shot 35 episodes and the show was Nickelodeon's highest-rated series, but it was unclear if it would be renewed for a second season. There were

reports of discord on the set, including tension between Ariana and her co-star Jennette McCurdy. *Deadline* had reported in April that 'word is both feel constrained at kids-focused Nickelodeon and are ready to move on'. A few months later, Nickelodeon announced *Sam & Cat* would be concluding after its first season finished airing on 17 July. Rumours of a feud between Ariana and McCurdy continued after the cancellation, although neither actress ever confirmed if there was an actual conflict between them. McCurdy later told *E! News*, 'Ariana and I were and are extremely close and very like-minded in a lot of different ways and then, sort of as the show dissolved, everybody wanted to find some sort of hidden meaning in

our relationship. Some like drama and I think we butted heads at times but in a very sisterly way. She knows me so well and I know her so well that I think it was unfortunate that things kind of got misconstrued.'

Once *Sam & Cat* had officially wrapped, Ariana was finally free to pursue her music career. It was either very fortuitous or very well-planned that her next single, 'Break Free', dropped only weeks before Ariana herself broke free of her commitment to Nickelodeon. For the buoyant song, the singer again worked with Martin and Kotecha, this time tapping EDM artist Zedd as her musical collaborator. Zedd told *MTV News* he had wanted to work with Ariana after seeing her

perform at a showcase for artists signed to Universal Music Group. 'I didn't know who it was, and I loved the voice, so I was like, "Whoever is on right now I want to make a song with,"' he said. 'And I figured it out: It was Ariana.' The soaring, anthemic electronic song marked a distinct departure for Ariana, although she admitted that delving into a new genre sparked her inspiration. 'I never thought I'd do an EDM song, but that was an eye-opening experience, and now all I want to do is dance,' she told *Billboard*.

The lyrics on 'Break Free' were empowering but somewhat nonsensical, which Ariana said she fought about with Martin in the studio. 'Max was like, "It's funny – just do it!"' she said in an interview with *TIME*. 'I know it's funny and silly, but grammatically incorrect things make me cringe sometimes.' Ultimately, embracing Martin's sensibility was liberating for Ariana, reflecting the theme of the single itself. She explained that the line saying she wanted to 'die alive' was a cheeky way of not taking life too seriously. 'It means life is so short – there's no reason to not enjoy it and there's no reason you should be anything but yourself,' she said. A music video inspired by space movies like *Barbarella* and *Star Wars*

and featuring an appearance from Zedd followed the single's release. By that October, the video had earned more than 100 million views on YouTube.

Only a few weeks after 'Break Free' hit the airwaves, Ariana joined forces with British pop singer Jessie J and popular rapper Nicki Minaj for 'Bang Bang.' The promotional single was released ahead of *My Everything* and was also part of Jessie J's forthcoming album, *Sweet Talker*. Ariana initially recorded a version of 'Bang Bang' with Martin and Kotecha early in the process of making *My Everything*. She wasn't a fan of the result, according to Wendy Goldstein, head of Urban A&R at Republic Records. 'It was written for Ariana,' Goldstein said to *Billboard*. 'She cut it, and she hated it.' Goldstein felt the song had potential, so she had Jessie J and Minaj add their vocals without telling Ariana. Ariana admitted that she didn't think about 'Bang Bang' again until she was in the office of Republic Records chairman and CEO Monte Lipman, who Goldstein had tasked with convincing Ariana to release the song. He played her the new version, which now featured the additional vocals. The ploy worked. 'I was like, "Oh my God, this is amazing,"' Ariana recounted to *Grammy.com*.

'I was like, "Am I about to have a **DUET** with Jessie J?" And then Nicki came in and I almost had a heart attack.'

'And then the second verse came in and it was me and I was like, "Am I about to have a duet with Jessie J?" And then Nicki came in and I almost had a heart attack.'

Although the singers recorded their parts separately, the song ultimately represented a collaboration between the three artists. Each lent her own strength and songwriting to the song, resulting in an empowering combination of their specific talents. 'It kind of became this female anthem, like a girl band,' Jessie J told *Rolling Stone*. 'Not a feature, but a moment where all of us can really show off what makes us us. And do it together.' Ariana, Jessie J and Minaj didn't actually meet until the music video shoot with director Hannah Lux Davis in Los Angeles. The video featured Ariana wearing her signature high ponytail and a tight, two-piece ensemble, performing her vocals in an intimate bedroom setting, again revealing a more mature side to the singer. 'We were just so giddy, all of us,' Jessie J told *Glamour* of filming the cinematic video. 'I remember us taking a selfie. I remember going, "I literally feel like I'm a fan in the back of the picture." I just remember laughing. Ariana's one of the funniest people ever [...] It was such a celebratory moment.'

'Bang Bang' was nominated for Best Pop Duo/Group Performance at the Grammys and Best Collaboration at the MTV Video Music Awards, although Grande seemed to want to leave it in the rearview mirror once the promotion had finished. Several years later, when preparing to tour on her fourth album, *Sweetener*, Ariana quipped that she wasn't interested in performing the song anymore. 'Lots of new materiaaaaal + oldies (the oldies we like),' she tweeted of what she planned to play on the road. 'I mean unless y'all wanna

hear bang bang again.' One of the singer's followers quickly replied, 'Girl, I never wanna hear that shit again.' Ariana concurred, 'Thank God. Cant wait to show this to my team.' It didn't help that Jessie J took credit for the song, mistakenly assuming that it was written for her. That miscommunication resulted in a public spat between her and Minaj and an apology from Jessie J in 2021. She wrote on Instagram that she had only just found out that Ariana was part of the writing process on 'Bang Bang.' 'Sorry Ari,' Jessie J acknowledged. 'I never knew. Wild.' Minaj joined Ariana onstage during her headlining set at Coachella in 2019 to perform the song – without Jessie J.

On 22 August 2014, Ariana released *My Everything*, her second album. Although the singles leading up to the LP were an eclectic mix of genres, the album itself adhered closely to the singer's preferred 90s-throwback R&B vibe. She had teased several of the tracks online, including the LP's fourth single, 'Love Me Harder,' which featured The Weeknd, and 'Best Mistake,' her second collaboration with Big Sean. The praise came in hard and fast, although not every critic was convinced by the featured vocalists, who also included Childish Gambino and A$AP Ferg, or by ballads such as 'Just a Little Bit of Your Heart.' Still, most agreed that the songs reflected an emotional growth spurt for the former Nickelodeon star. 'It's a confident, intelligent, brazen pop statement, mixing bubblegum diva vocals with EDM break beats,' *Rolling Stone* wrote in a review, adding, 'Grande doesn't have much interest in wuss ballads where she plays the victim – she's an I'm-so-moving-on type, which is what gives her voice its emotional kick.'

My Everything revealed a version of Ariana who refused to settle and who embraced

playfulness even in the face of heartbreak or disappointment. Her vocals, as noted by many critics, were as strong as ever although lyrically some of the album lacked the desired sense of get-to-know-you depth from Ariana. Fans wanted the lyrics to reveal more about her life on a personal level but they would have to wait for her to be ready to divulge that in her songs. Still, shortly after the release of the album, Ariana confirmed she was dating Big Sean, who had previously called off his engagement to actress Naya Rivera. It wasn't clear when their relationship had started, nor whether it had impacted the overall writing of the album, although he was responsible for the uncredited whispering vocals on 'Problem.' 'He is one of the most amazing men in the whole world, and that includes my grandfather and my brother,' Ariana told *The Telegraph* in October 2014 when pressed by the interviewer. 'I think the world of him, and he's an amazing person. That's kind of all there is to it.' Their joint track, 'Best Mistake,' centred on a couple with a troubled relationship – likely not what the pair was experiencing at the time. The piano-led ballad was sultry and intimate, despite its

'I want to inspire
my fans to be...

BOOSTING

each other up
rather than tearing
each other down...'

tempestuous theme. *SPIN* called it 'classic Grande, eschewing any of the bells and whistles that she's fond of, instead focusing entirely on her carefully sung vocals and the quiet piano line in the song's background.'

In September 2014, Ariana appeared as the musical guest on the season premiere of late-night comedy show *Saturday Night Live* alongside host Chris Pratt. It was a huge opportunity for the singer, who was just 21 years old at the time. Not only did she perform 'Break Free' and 'Love Me Harder', but Ariana also gamely appeared as children's character She-Ra in a sketch titled 'He-Man and Lion-O'. In the sketch, a young boy named Danny wished his action figures to life on his birthday. The now-living toys didn't understand anything about the real world, a premise that was ripe for sexualized comedy. To showcase 'Break Free' as the musical guest, Ariana opted for a sparse stage production, beginning the dance tune as an evocative ballad and then breaking into choreography as the beat picked up. She wore black cat ears over her ponytail, an accessory that became a favourite for Ariana in that era. She donned them again for 'Love Me Harder', during which she was joined onstage mid-song by The Weeknd to share vocals on the emotional track.

Around the end of 2014, the press began to focus more negatively on Ariana. In December, *Life & Style* released a dubious report that claimed Ariana insisted on being carried everywhere. An unnamed source told the outlet, 'Her new rule is that she has to be carried – literally carried like a baby – when she doesn't feel like walking.' This was, of course, untrue. Ariana later explained that her tour manager had carried her once and the rumour had spiralled out of control. 'I'll tell you

what happened,' she told James Corden during an episode of *Carpool Karaoke* in 2018. 'There was a picture of me being carried by my tour manager because I had just shot a video in pointe shoes, and I posted it because I thought it was cute. My toes were bleeding.' Ariana understood the ridiculousness of the claims and poked fun at herself on *Carpool Karaoke* by hopping on Corden's back to go into a Starbucks. Even if some of the media attention was unwanted, it was clear that Ariana was becoming a notable public figure who warranted constant coverage from the press. This wouldn't be the only time Ariana was subjected to criticism, whether it was based on truth or not. And soon, she would have an actual controversy to contend with.

To promote *My Everything*, Ariana embarked on her first world tour. The Honeymoon Tour kicked off on 25 February 2015 in Independence, Missouri and continued through late October, when the tour wrapped in São Paulo, Brazil. Ariana took the preparation for the tour very seriously, just as she had everything else in her career. She undertook several months of rehearsals with her dancers and her seven-piece band, pushing herself to the brink. 'these rehearsals are kicking my ass but i love it,' she tweeted in January 2015. 'really want to make this show the best I'm capable of.' She teased fans with footage of the rehearsals, a performance of 'One Last Time' and a clip of a conversation between herself and her recently deceased grandfather. 'Music – you want to do something in music? Go ahead and do it,' he told her in the video, which she played each night on the tour. 'Don't let them challenge you; don't let them intimidate you. Do your thing, that's the only way to do it.'

Ariana enlisted Emmy Award-winning costume designer Marina Toybina to design the tour's costumes. 'We were able to work closely together, collaborating on all aspects of the initial and the final design stages in order to accommodate and best execute Ariana's creative vision for her first world tour,' Toybina told *The Hollywood Reporter*. Toybina designed seven looks, including a sequinned onesie with a flowing lavender skirt covered in flowers and a 1920s-inspired silver flapper dress. Ariana's signature cat ears popped up multiple times. 'I am always drawn to things that are slightly retro and sort of, like, throwback,' Ariana explained of her style in an interview with radio station Power 106 Los Angeles. 'I love an animal ear.' Many fans assumed the ears were a nod to Cat Valentine, although Ariana said it was more about her love of being a cat for Halloween. 'They're just fun,' she noted.

The opening night of The Honeymoon Tour felt momentous, everything Ariana had been anticipating for years. Officially, she hadn't been able to tour due to her obligations to Nickelodeon, and The Honeymoon Tour represented weeks of hard work. UK band Rixton and Cashmere Cat opened the show.

During his set, Cashmere Cat debuted one of the tracks he had produced for Ariana to feature vocals on, 'Adore', with Ariana surprising fans when she came out to sing the lyrics. During her own set, Ariana admitted to being nervous 'but in a good way', although critics observed that she seemed as confident as ever. 'The show at the sold-out Independence Events Center was an extravagant mix of music, dance, lasers, videos, pyrotechnics, and costume changes, akin to the kinds of audio-visual spectacles delivered by fellow pop-divas like Katy Perry and Britney Spears,' the *Kansas City Star* wrote in its review. Several reviewers called out Ariana's incorporation of MiMU Gloves, a technology designed by Imogen Heap, as a distraction from her impressive vocals. At the end of the night, Ariana was relieved and gratified by the response from fans, sharing a thank you with fans in a video blog.

After 26 shows in North America, Ariana continued the tour in Europe – her first time touring overseas. She returned to North America for another leg of dates over the summer before jetting to Asia in August and then back to the US, Mexico and South America. Ariana performed 88 concerts in total, keeping the set list largely consistent throughout. Occasionally, the singer was joined by a special guest. In Detroit, Big Sean surprised fans to duet on 'Best Mistake' and 'Right There', and Justin Bieber showed up in Miami and Los Angeles to duet 'Love Me Harder'. Towards the end of the tour, Ariana debuted her first fragrance, Ari by Ariana Grande, which she created with Firmenich's Frank Voelkl. She launched it alongside a campaign dubbed 'Be You', which encouraged fans to be themselves – a message Ariana

herself embodied. 'I want to inspire my fans to be unapologetically themselves, celebrating our differences, boosting each other up rather than tearing each other down and meeting society's ridiculous standard of beauty and perfection,' she told *Women's Wear Daily*. 'It's really nice now and then to be reminded that being yourself is more than enough. You're totally perfect. That's so cheesy to say, but it's true.'

One of the backup dancers on The Honeymoon Tour was Ricky Alvarez. Ariana and Alvarez became close on the road and began dating over the summer of 2015. That July, the couple became the subject of controversy when *TMZ* acquired security footage of Ariana and a group of her friends hanging out in a doughnut shop, Wolfee

Donuts, in Lake Elsinore, California. In the footage, Ariana snuck a lick of one of the powdered-sugar doughnuts on the counter and Alvarez followed suit. The singer did it again later in the video on another tray of doughnuts before she and Alvarez kissed. In the clip, Ariana could be heard criticizing her country, saying, 'I hate Americans. I hate America.'

The video quickly went viral. In the wake of the incident, Ariana attempted to explain herself on Twitter, noting that she was 'proud to be an American' but felt 'very upset' about their eating habits. The footage led to a police investigation and Ariana eventually shared a contrite video apologizing for her behaviour. 'Seeing a video of yourself behaving poorly,

that you have no idea was taken, is such a rude awakening that you don't know what to do – I was so disgusted with myself,' she said. Ariana ultimately didn't face any charges, but it did impact her reputation, with many public figures criticizing her on social media and in the press. Ariana accepted the criticism and tried to move on. 'I'm 22 years old, I'm human, I still got a lot to learn,' she said in her apology.

As she wowed fans nightly on The Honeymoon Tour, Ariana continued to split her focus between various pursuits. She had already begun working on new music, and she wanted to take advantage of an opportunity to return to acting. For several years now, Ariana had been focused solely on her singing career. She had released two albums and embarked

on her first world tour, fulfilling her dreams of becoming a pop star. But she had also had her big break onscreen, and it was only natural that she would pursue another acting role if it felt right. She made her return to TV in Ryan Murphy's *Scream Queens*, a satirical slasher series that took place in the Kappa Kappa Tau sorority. Ariana was cast as Sonya Herfmann, also known as Chanel #2 because she was one of several followers of Emma Roberts' bossy sorority sister Chanel Oberlin.

Murphy created the show with Brad Falchuk and Ian Brennan, and said they were inspired by the 80s and early-90s slasher genre. Murphy told *Entertainment Weekly* that Ariana joined the cast after he pitched her the idea. 'I met her and she had been a big fan of

American Horror Story,' he said. 'We have to carve out amounts of time for her but I love her. She's great and funny and she loves the genre of it.' Ariana explained to *Extra* she was a 'huge fan' of all of Murphy's work. 'When I got the chance to meet with him I was like, "Literally, whatever you want me to do I'm down,"' she said. 'I was like, "I'll play any role. I'll be the first one to die. The villain. I'll be anything you want." I was so excited when this opportunity came about.' The series began filming in New Orleans in the spring of 2015, ahead of The Honeymoon Tour, and continued throughout the summer. Ariana originally signed on for one episode only, but Murphy told *E! News* that she 'loved the process so much that she wanted to do more.' Scheduling around her tour was challenging, and Murphy

had to juggle Ariana's concert obligations as well as those of singer Nick Jonas. 'It's a little crazy and sometimes we have to shoot on the weekends and fly people in and move things around, but I always think that it's worth it,' Murphy said. 'For the most part, these roles one hundred per cent were made for these people, and I think you can feel it in the way they perform.'

Scream Queens premiered on 22 September 2015 to great anticipation. The shocking, bloody pilot episode culminated with Ariana's character being murdered – a surprise death for someone so famous. But that wasn't the end for Chanel #2. Ariana played the character's dead body for her funeral and later appeared haunting Chanel #1's dreams. The show got mixed reviews, although Ariana's

'To do something completely different, just a complete

180,

it's really fun.'

death scene and her comic ability were widely praised. While her role wasn't particularly expansive, Ariana enjoyed her return to TV. She told *Extra* that taking time off from the tour was a 'nice change of pace'. 'To do something completely different, just a complete 180, it's really fun,' she said. It also made her miss acting. 'I want to do more,' she admitted. 'I feel like after doing these couple of episodes I'm sort of wanting to do a little bit more now.'

But acting wouldn't be on the cards for Ariana again for a few more years. She concluded a very successful 2015 with her second holiday EP, *Christmas & Chill*. Produced by Tommy Brown, Mr. Franks, The Magi and Travis Sayles, the six-track EP featured original songs recorded in Ariana's home studio in Los Angeles in less than a week. Ariana described the experience to fans as 'a long, productive slumber party'. The music was R&B-inspired, with a festive energy and innuendo-laced lyrics. The release stood out for fans as a rare Christmas album that had original tunes instead of classic covers. *Billboard* later named the EP one of 'The 21 Best Christmas Albums of the 21st Century', writing, 'This isn't your parents' holiday fare.' It was a fitting way to close the year and reflected what might come next from Ariana: more new music, more live shows and many more opportunities to express herself.

3

Love Me
HARDER

DANGEROUS WOMAN, MANCHESTER and ONE LOVE

By the time Ariana released her second album, *My Everything*, the singer had built incredible momentum. It was clear she was going to do everything in her power to keep it going. While promoting *My Everything*, Ariana began to hint at a third album. In the late summer of 2015, she teased her next project, then titled *Moonlight*, on Twitter, suggesting that it might arrive the following month, 'babies i'm so excited for the nearby future... (also embracing and loving the present)... but I'm really effing excited for the near future,' she wrote. 'personally...... I consider October "nearby future". In September, she announced a single called 'Focus' during an appearance on *The Tonight Show*. She previewed the track in October in a commercial for her debut fragrance, Ari by Ariana Grande, and on 30 October 2015 'Focus' arrived alongside a slick music video directed by Hannah Lux Davis.

Grande co-wrote 'Focus' with her longtime collaborator Savan Kotecha, Peter Svensson and the song's producers, Ilya Salmanzadeh and Max Martin. The brash pop single evoked the singer's love for nostalgic musical styles, incorporating big-band horns and thumping percussion. The male backing vocals were courtesy of actor Jamie Foxx, a surprise inclusion Ariana revealed only after its release. 'We were thinking, "Who should say this part? What's the right fit?"' she told *Entertainment Tonight*. 'And we were just sort of like, "Jamie Foxx. That would be crazy."' Her team had reached out to Foxx's and, to Ariana's

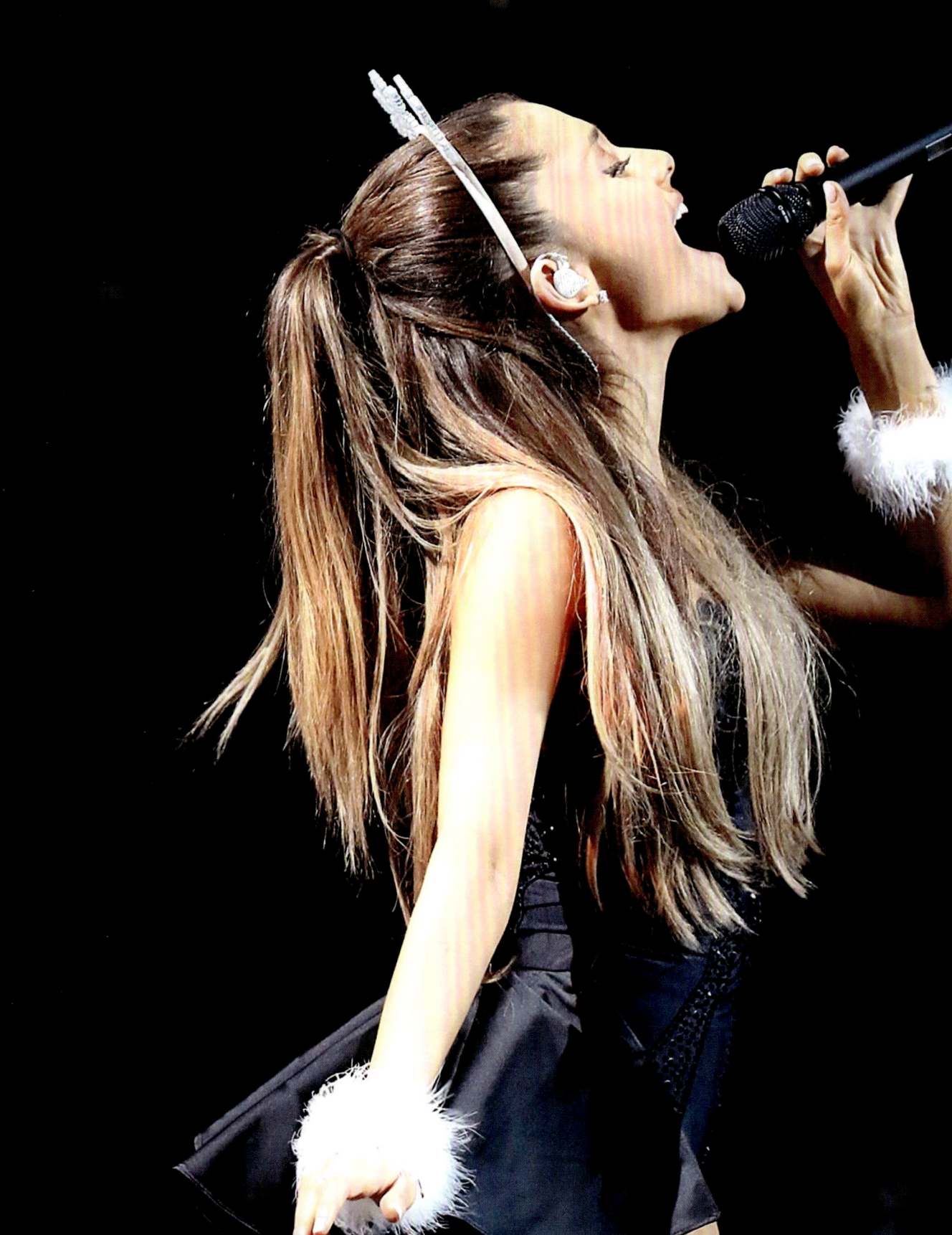

excitement, he had agreed to come on board. 'It was awesome,' she said. 'He definitely added that whole James Brown feel that we were going for.'

The single felt somewhat experimental for Ariana at the time, recalling her similarly upbeat track 'Problem' while also pushing into new sonic territory. On the soaring chorus, she proclaimed that she was here to stay and would not buy into the discourse surrounding her, negative or positive. People could talk, she asserted, but she was going to keep being herself and working hard. 'The first line of "Focus" is: "I know what I came to do and that ain't gonna change,"' Ariana explained in a video she released on YouTube. 'What I came here to do in this world is not only to entertain but to love, to share, to listen, to improve, to learn, to share music, to share experience, to share feelings, to make people feel happy and empowered.' She added, 'When I say, "Focus on me", I'm not asking to be the centre of attention. I'm not asking you to focus on my face or my clothes or my body or my singing voice. By "focus on me", I literally mean focus on me. Focus on what I'm all about and what I believe in.' It shouldn't be about appearance, gender, sexuality or skin colour, she said, adding that she hoped people would 'focus on each other on a soul level.' 'The more we realize how much we have in common, the more we listen to each other, the more one we become,' she concluded.

Although the song debuted at No. 7 on the *Billboard* Hot 100 chart, the reception was lukewarm. 'It was calculated to a fault, too polished for a time when pop's biggest stars, particularly its women, are letting their flaws bleed into the music,' *Vulture* noted. But for Ariana, the overt comparison to 'Problem' was intentional. She described the song to

Entertainment Tonight as 'the perfect transition record from the last album to the new album because it sounds like "Problem 2.0". It sounds like the goodbye to the last album and hello to the new album.' Ultimately, though, 'Focus' wasn't included on Ariana's third album, which eventually became *Dangerous Woman*. Instead of releasing more music after wrapping The Honeymoon Tour, Ariana returned to the studio to finish the album. 'I'm excited for the next couple of months to not only finish [*Moonlight*] but to have actual undivided time where I can really just focus on the music,' she told UK radio station KISS. 'I just feel like once I finally get the time to really dedicate myself 100 per cent, I'm going to maybe outdo what we've already done.'

In January 2016, Ariana appeared on *Jimmy Kimmel Live*. She told the talkshow host that one particular track had caused her to re-evaluate the entire album, including its title. 'As we're wrapping things up, of course I've been writing and singing, we're at the final stretch,' she said. 'Now there's this other song that has thrown me for a whirlwind and I love it so much, it's changed everything.' The following month, Ariana made it official: *Moonlight* was now titled *Dangerous Woman*. The album's name referenced Nawal El Saadawi's 1975 novel *Woman at Point Zero*, which Ariana felt encapsulated a woman who was not afraid to be honest and take a stand. The album's cover art also made a statement; it showcased Ariana wearing a black latex bunny mask, a persona the singer dubbed 'Super Bunny'. '[She] is my superhero, or supervillain – whatever I'm feeling on the day,' Grande told *Billboard*. 'Whenever I doubt myself or question choices I know in my gut are right – because other people are telling me other things – I'm

like, "What would that bad bitch Super Bunny do?" She helps me call the shots.'

The first official song Ariana shared from the album was the sultry title track, 'Dangerous Woman'. It aptly previewed the entire collection of songs, which she described as 'a little darker and sexier and more mature.' The mid-tempo, edgy single, produced by Martin and Johan Carlsson, saw Ariana embracing her strength. 'Before, I think I was afraid to be myself and make decisions and speak out about things I'm passionate about because I thought it would make me experience some of the stereotypes that women in power often face,' she said in an interview with Ryan Seacrest.

Several critics compared 'Dangerous Woman' to the theme song from a James Bond film, commenting on its seductive vocals and propulsive beat. 'It is, without a doubt, the most mature piece of music she's released to date,' *SPIN* wrote, calling the song 'smart, sexy, captivating, and sung to total perfection.' *Rolling Stone* named it one of the 30 best songs of the year to date. Indeed, the song heralded what was to come from Ariana and helped to establish that she was, at 22 years old, now fully grown-up.

Ariana was tapped as both the host and the musical guest of *Saturday Night Live* on 12 March 2016. She took the opportunity to perform 'Dangerous Woman' and album cut 'Be Alright', but also got to show off her comedic skills and her talent for mimicry during many sketches. Her performance brought in rave reviews, including from filmmaker Steven Spielberg, who texted *SNL*'s creator Lorne Michaels to say how impressed he was. Ariana also addressed the fallout from the doughnut-licking scandal in her monologue, showing just how self-aware she really was. 'I was just so

'There's this other SONG that has thrown me for a whirlwind and I love it so much, it's changed everything.'

happy to be able to make fun of myself,' Grande told *Billboard* later. 'If you think you're laughing at me, I promise I laughed first.'

Originally, Ariana planned to release two music videos for 'Dangerous Woman' because the single made her feel two completely different ways. 'It makes me feel sexy and glamorous – I wanted to do a simpler more glam-themed video and then I wanted to do another video because it makes me feel like a super version of myself in a way,' she told *Idolator*. She ended up releasing only one video due to time constraints. The intimate, cinematic clip, directed by the Young Astronauts, showcased her in black lingerie posing and singing in front of a curtain and on a white couch. Like the song itself, the video was grown-up and sophisticated, again indicating the direction in which Ariana wanted to go and how she hoped to be perceived.

Several more tracks followed ahead of the album's release in May. Along with 'Be Alright', which Ariana had performed on *SNL*, she debuted a collaboration with Lil Wayne titled 'Let Me Love You'. The silky, evocative R&B number was the first song Ariana wrote for the album with the help of her pal Victoria Monét. It also marked Ariana's first duet with Lil Wayne, who had famously referenced her on his 2015 song 'London Roads'. In his verse on 'Let Me Love You', Lil Wayne signified Ariana's newfound maturity, memorably rapping 'goodbye to the good girl'. 'It's one of my favourite verses of his ever,' Ariana affirmed during an interview on BBC Radio 1Xtra. On 6 May 2016, only a few weeks before the album dropped, Ariana dropped 'Into You', the most standout song off the LP so far. The dance-ready track centred on Ariana professing her emotion for a romantic partner and asking him to pay more attention to her. Stop talking, she proclaimed, and make a move. The chorus seemingly referenced two prior hits: Elvis Presley's 1968 song 'A Little Less Conversation' and Mariah Carey's 2008 single 'Touch My Body'. It was hooky and irresistible. Critics dubbed it 'brazen' and 'scandalous', and *Rolling Stone* noted that the song was 'primed for dance floor make out sessions'.

As a whole, *Dangerous Woman* was a declaration of empowerment, adulthood and

independence. It continued Ariana's love of singing about relationships, but also solidified her as the leading character in her life. 'Moonlight', the album's opening number and original namesake, was inspired by Ariana's boyfriend of the time, Ricky Alvarez. Monét revealed to *Billboard* that the song got its original title from a name Alvarez called Ariana shortly after their first kiss. 'He waited to kiss her for a long time, and she was really impressed,' Monét said. 'He's such a gentleman, and the song is a great little bookmark of the start of their relationship.' 'Side to Side', a reggae-pop track, featured Nicki Minaj and was more blatantly sexual. The NSFW song was about spending hours in bed with a lover – a foolproof way for the former Nickelodeon star to assert her womanhood. The song was co-written and co-produced by hitmaker Jack Antonoff, who was dating actress and *Girls* creator Lena Dunham at the time. After the album's release, Dunham tweeted, 'Jack just explained that the song "Side to Side" is about getting railed so hard you can't walk.' Ariana confirmed this in an interview with *MTV News*: 'That whole song is about riding leading to soreness.' She was no longer the young girl from *Victorious*, but a fully fledged woman – and hopefully a dangerous one at that.

Around the release of *Dangerous Woman*, Ariana announced she planned to tour again. In September, shortly after a performance at the MTV Video Music Awards alongside Minaj, she revealed the dates for the first leg of the *Dangerous Woman Tour*. It was scheduled to kick off on 3 February 2017 in Phoenix, Arizona and continue around North America through to mid-April. 'I'm very excited,' she told Jimmy Fallon on *The Tonight Show*. 'I can't wait to get on the road again. There will be more dates

coming.' Soon after, she announced the international tour dates, which included stops in Europe, South America, Asia and Australia. A lot of planning went into the visuals. Ariana collaborated with stylist Law Roach and designer Bryan Hearns to create a series of stage looks inspired equally by Audrey Hepburn, TLC and street style. The tour costumes evoked Ariana's classic silhouette – high-waisted bodysuits, shorts, skirts and crop-top shirts – but also pushed the boundaries with leather, denim and sweatshirt fabrics. Hearns described the aesthetic to *Billboard* as 'confident, feminine and dangerous.' 'She's trying to do a different direction with her style, and this tour kind of encompasses all of that,' he confirmed.

The high-energy tour opened with 'Be Alright', with Ariana clad in a high-neck skirted black bodysuit. It took place over four acts, each with its own vibe, and saw Ariana fully owning her talent on the stage. Despite its slick production, which included stationary bikes for 'Side to Side' and a shower of money-adorned confetti during 'Greedy', critics and fans agreed that the best moments came when Ariana let her voice carry the show. 'It's a pristine showcase of her immense vocal talent, crafted under the watchful eye of chief pop machinist Max Martin', *The Washington Post* wrote in a review of her performance at the Verizon Center. *Las Vegas Weekly* agreed: 'Grande's burly, soulful vibrato and wide range remain the star of her show, and she's at her best when it's just her, a microphone and her band – especially when she performs ballads'. It was a celebratory tour intended to bridge Ariana's earlier albums with her latest work, and it felt big and boisterous. During a mid-show interlude, the screen provocatively displayed feminist words, including 'empowered', 'grounded' and 'human'. The phrase 'not asking for it' repeated across the screen, the assertion of an important truth for Ariana.

The North American leg of the tour concluded successfully. Ariana took a break before flying to Stockholm, where she began the European leg on 8 May 2017. She performed concerts in Oslo, Herning and Amsterdam and then headed to the UK and Ireland for shows in Birmingham, Dublin and Manchester. It was a whirlwind experience for the singer, who was finally getting to live out her touring dream with her highly successful third album. But Ariana's life and career changed forever on 22 May 2017, a day that would divide her existence into 'before' and 'after'.

Moments after Ariana left the stage following her performance at Manchester's Manchester Arena, a terrorist detonated a nail bomb in the venue's foyer. The impact killed 23 people, including the bomber, and injured more than 800 others. The youngest fatality was only eight years old. The bomb went off just after pink balloons had fallen from the ceiling, a visual disconnect between the uplifting ebullience of Ariana's tour and the grim reality of what had just transpired. Ariana, experiencing the chaos from backstage with her dancers and crew, was in shock. She was physically unharmed, but mentally and emotionally shattered. A few hours later, she shared a message on Twitter. 'broken', she wrote. 'from the bottom of my heart, i am so so sorry. i don't have words'.

The days that followed were a struggle. Ariana suspended the upcoming dates of her *Dangerous Woman* tour and flew home to Florida. Mac Miller, her boyfriend at the time, was photographed meeting her at the airport in Boca Raton. For two days, Ariana cried and barely spoke. She had no idea if she would ever be able to perform again. She later admitted to *British Vogue* that she had suffered from

post-traumatic stress disorder in the wake of the attack and continued to struggle with discussing the bombing 'because so many people have suffered such severe, tremendous loss'. 'I know those families and my fans, and everyone there experienced a tremendous amount of it as well,' she explained. 'Time is the biggest thing. I feel like I shouldn't even be talking about my own experience – like I shouldn't even say anything. I don't think I'll ever know how to talk about it and not cry.'

The public response to the bombing was immense. In the aftermath, Queen Elizabeth II shared a statement, writing, 'The whole nation has been shocked […] I know I speak for everyone in expressing my deepest sympathy to all who have been affected by this dreadful event and especially to the families and friends of those who have died or were injured.' The following week, on 25 May 2017, the UK held a minute of silence for the victims. A song by Manchester band Oasis, 'Don't Look Back in Anger,' played afterwards. On the same day, Queen Elizabeth II visited Royal Manchester Children's Hospital to meet with young survivors. Vigils were held across the country and many international leaders and politicians shared their condolences.

Although Ariana was battling PTSD, she felt she couldn't keep hiding. A few days after flying home to Florida, she got into bed with her mom in the middle of the night. 'It was two or three in the morning,' Joan recounted to *ELLE*. 'She crawled into bed and said, "Mom, let's be honest, I'm never not going to sing again. But I'm not going to sing again until I sing in Manchester first."' They called Scooter Braun, Ariana's manager, to discuss how Ariana could help. 'At first I had to slow my mind down because Ariana – rightfully so – she didn't know if she could ever go on stage again,' Braun told *Billboard*. 'And then two days after she called

me and she goes, "Look, I need to do something. I keep thinking about it and if I don't do something I feel like they might have died in vain. So what's the idea?'"

Braun and Ariana conceived a benefit concert to take place in Manchester. At first, there was significant doubt from the music industry. Braun got a lot of negative responses. He was constantly told, 'It's too soon.' 'We didn't care,' he said. 'The first thing I did was reach out to the family liaison [team], explain the idea and say, "I just want to know if I have the support of the families." The families came back with an overwhelming yes. I got that answer within 24 hours and the moment that happened we were on a mission. You couldn't tell us no! Soon, other artists began to say yes. It wouldn't just be Ariana taking the stage in Manchester. It would be a community of global artists coming together to support the city in the wake of an unimaginable tragedy; it took Braun only

12 days to pull together the event by calling in favour after favour. Ultimately, he enlisted an incredible array of acts, including Coldplay, Take That, Justin Bieber, Robbie Williams, Niall Horan, Black Eyed Peas, Marcus Mumford, Imogen Heap, Mac Miller, Miley Cyrus and Oasis's Liam Gallagher.

On 30 May, Ariana announced the benefit concert, One Love Manchester. It would take place on 4 June 2017 at Manchester's Old Trafford stadium, and it would raise money for the We Love Manchester Emergency Fund, which had been set up by Manchester City Council and the British Red Cross. Ariana offered free tickets for anyone who had been at the Manchester Arena show, with the rest of the tickets going on sale to the wider public. She acknowledged how important it was to her to be present with the community and with her fans in the midst of their grief. 'I don't want to go the rest of the year without being able to see and hold and uplift my fans,' she affirmed on Twitter when the concert was announced. 'I'll be returning to the incredibly brave city of Manchester to spend time with my fans and to have a benefit concert in honour of and to raise money for the victims and their families.' Paid tickets sold out in just 23 minutes.

On 3 June 2017, a second terrorist attack took place on London Bridge. The attackers killed eight people and injured many more. The entire country was shaken and scared. Braun expected the other artists on the One Love Manchester lineup to cancel. 'They could have easily said, "Hey, let's just give it some time,"' he later recalled to *Billboard*. 'And every single one of them not only said, "We're in," some of them called me to say, "You're not cancelling, right? Don't cancel."' Braun admitted to having a moment of hesitation himself, but said he knew he was doing the right thing by not cancelling One Love Manchester after the second attack, asserting that he had a responsibility to honour not only Manchester, but also London. 'The point of these attacks is to make us be scared to live our lives and the best way we can honor those affected is to be defiant to evil,' he told *Music Week*.

A few days before the concert, Ariana surprised patients at Royal Manchester Children's Hospital, including eight-year-old Lily Harrison, who had been in the hospital along with her mother since the attack. The singer brought flowers and Harrods teddy bears and spent the day speaking with the victims. 'Ariana asked her what her favourite song was and Lily chose one of her less popular songs – she looked quite impressed that Lily hadn't chosen one of the big hits,' Lily's father Adam Harrison told *The Guardian*. He added that Ariana's presence helped his daughter. 'For the first

three or four days after the attack she didn't speak, other than to answer yes or no,' he said. 'Now she's getting back to her old self and has even watched a video [her mum] took of her singing along to Ariana at the concert where all of this happened.'

Ariana and her team also met with the families of the victims, one by one. It was extremely difficult. Ariana felt the loss of each fan individually. 'After the first family I had to help her, she was distraught and I was lost,' Braun recounted on podcast *Big Questions With Cal Fussman*. 'It was beyond tough. But every single time we got down we reminded each other we get to go home. Our loved ones are still going to be there [...] We didn't have the right to be so sad we couldn't continue.' The mother of 15-year-old victim Olivia Campbell was the final meeting. 'We were talking with her about the show and she told me what songs were Olivia's favourites and she said, "We need to play the hits. That's what Olivia would have wanted,"' Braun told *Billboard*. 'That gave Ariana the courage to say, "This needs to also be a celebration of people."'

Getting back on stage, particularly in Manchester, was admittedly terrifying. But, as Ariana told *ABC News* in 2018, her fans and the city itself inspired her to try. She didn't want to 'recoil and go away', even though her initial reaction was to never perform again. 'I was like, "I love ya'll, I can't do it,"' she recalled. But on the day of One Love Manchester, Ariana got dressed, put her hair in a ponytail and prepared to perform. Security at the venue was especially tight. A lot of extra precautions were taken to keep the crowd safe and to ensure fans felt comfortable being there. Braun was worried no one would come after what had happened in London, especially as the BBC was

Fly to the
Angels. Heaven
awaits your heart
and flowers bloom
in your name.
R.I.P

'Tonight
is all about
LOVE,
am I right?'

broadcasting the entire concert directly into people's homes. But 50,000 people showed up at Old Trafford. Many had T-shirts and signs with hopeful messages, and while sad emotions were present, the overall feeling was joy. Only 13 days had passed since the bombing, but fans were determined to stay strong and carry on.

Marcus Mumford opened the concert with a moment of silence to honour the victims of the attacks in Manchester and London. After the sombre tribute, the musician, standing centre stage, urged, 'Let's not be afraid.' He performed a solo version of Mumford & Sons' 'Timshel', a song about not being alone in the face of sadness. In all, the concert lasted more than three hours and featured performances by Take That, Robbie Williams, Pharrell Williams, Katy Perry, Niall Horan, Coldplay, Justin Bieber, and more. Early on in the evening, Williams invited Miley Cyrus to join him for a lively rendition of his song 'Happy', an uplifting performance that encouraged the audience to feel free and joyous. 'As humans we should always be who we say we are,' Cyrus told the crowd after the song. 'And Ariana, I think, has proven that.'

Ariana waited until an hour into the concert to appear on stage. Braun introduced her with a series of thank yous for those putting on the show and for the first responders who had risked their lives after the attack. 'This is so beautiful,' he told the fans. 'You guys made that decision. You looked fear right in the face and you said, "No, we are Manchester and the world is watching."' As he finally welcomed Ariana, there were deafening screams from the crowd. Fittingly, Ariana began with 'Be Alright', smiling as she sang. The fans smiled back. She followed with another up-tempo number, 'Break Free', encouraging a wild singalong at the chorus. The

lyrics 'I'm stronger than I've been before' took on new meaning as she and her fans passionately brought their voices together in Old Trafford. Pink streamers fell to the floor as the song concluded and Ariana, overcome with emotion, covered her mouth with her hand.

The rest of the evening belonged to Ariana, even though she yielded the stage to other artists as the show continued to unfold. She and Victoria Monét collaborated on 'Better Days' and she took the microphone alongside Black-Eyed Peas for their hit 'Where Is the Love?' A group of Manchester teenagers from the Parrs Wood High School Choir joined her for 'My Everything', an emotional performance that left everyone in tears. Twelve-year-old choir member Natasha-Rose Seth sang the first verse, standing front and centre beside Ariana. As the rest of the choir and Ariana joined in, the young girl broke down. Ariana kept one arm around her until the end of the song, a gesture of kindness and support. She hugged choir members as they left the stage. 'Tonight is all about love, am I right?' she asked the audience before bringing out another significant guest: her boyfriend Mac Miller. Their duet of 'The Way' was one of the evening's most memorable highlights, a collaboration that would take on an added poignancy in the years that followed.

Midway through the evening, after performing Crowded House's 'Don't Dream It's Over' with Cyrus, Ariana acknowledged that her meeting with Olivia Campbell's mother two days prior had shifted her thinking about the concert. 'I had the pleasure of meeting Olivia's mommy a few days ago,' Ariana said. 'And as soon as I met her I started crying. She said [to] stop crying because Olivia wouldn't want me to cry and said Olivia would have wanted to hear the hits. We had a totally different show

planned and had a rehearsal but changed everything. Tonight has been filled with love and fun and bright energy, and I want to thank you for that.' Some of the songs were overtly emotional, like Ariana and Coldplay's cover of Oasis's 'Don't Look Back in Anger', a nod to Manchester. But other moments, like Liam Gallagher's surprise appearance, were hopeful and fun.

For the finale, Ariana invited all the participating artists on to the stage to perform 'One Last Time', the song she had played during the encore at Manchester Arena only two weeks earlier. The entire crowd sang along as Ariana held back tears. 'Manchester, I love you with all my heart,' she said before the closing chorus. 'Thank you so, so much.' But the rousing song wasn't the end. After everyone else exited, Ariana remained on stage with only a pianist. She closed the show with 'Over the Rainbow', an essential song from her childhood that represented hope. The track was her grandfather's favourite. 'He would always tell me to sing it in my concerts,' Ariana told *The Fader*. 'He would always say, "You know what you should end with? 'Over the Rainbow.'" And I never did it until that moment.'

The evening was a cathartic triumph for Ariana. She had made a decision to stand up to hatred and violence and darkness. 'You find the light eventually,' she explained later on *ABC News*. 'It's still a work in progress, but I think the sense of community that I saw in response to what happened was the best example of humanity.' Not only was One Love Manchester emotionally powerful, but it also raised a significant amount of money. By August, the We Love Manchester Emergency Fund had brought in more than £18 million ($23 million) through public donations and from the proceeds of the concert. The organization announced that the families of the twenty-two victims of the attack would receive £250,000 ($324,000) each. 'The payments will ensure the families benefit from the phenomenal outpouring of public support following the attack,' it said in a statement. The fund's chair of trustees, Sue Murphy, added, 'The city and the world responded with such extreme kindness, generosity and solidarity in the aftermath of the Manchester Arena attack.'

Ariana would be forever connected to Manchester. In June 2017, she became the first person to be named as an honorary citizen of the city due to her 'great many selfless acts

and demonstrations of community spirit' following the attack. 'This seems a fitting moment to update the way we recognize those who make noteworthy contributions to the life and success of our city,' Manchester City Council leader Sir Richard Leese told *BBC News*. 'We've all had cause to be incredibly proud of Manchester and the resilient and compassionate way in which the city, and all those associated with it, have responded to the terrible events of 22 May, with love and courage rather than hatred and fear. Ariana Grande exemplified this response. I think many people would already consider her an honorary Mancunian and we would be delighted, if the council approves the proposal, to make it official.' On a more personal level, Ariana tattooed a bee behind her left ear, a symbol of Manchester that she unveiled around the one-year anniversary of the attack. 'Forever,' she wrote in the caption when she revealed it on Instagram.

For almost a year, Ariana didn't speak publicly about the Manchester bombing. There was too much to express and it was still too raw. On 18 May 2018, the singer appeared on *The Tonight Show* to discuss her next album, *Sweetener*. Host Jimmy Fallon kept the conversation light, focusing on her new music and her upcoming performance at the *Billboard* Music Awards, but towards the end of the interview he brought up Manchester. He thanked her for showing up and entertaining people despite what she'd been through, and read a few lines of the message Ariana had shared with fans online following the attack. 'We won't let hate win,' he read. 'Our response to this violence must be to come closer together, to help each other, to love more, to sing louder, and to live more kindly and

generously than we did before.' Ariana didn't respond beyond saying, 'Thank you,' but Fallon's acknowledgement of her experience was an important step forward.

The late-night appearance opened the door for Ariana to feel comfortable doing more press and speaking up about her trauma in the months that followed. But in every interview, Ariana was clear: this was not about her. 'It's those families' [losses],' she told *Vogue*. 'It's their losses, and so it's hard to just let it all out without thinking about them reading this and reopening the memory for them.' Although she

was proud that One Love Manchester had raised a lot of money, and hoped it offered a feeling of love and unity, she also recognized the concert couldn't bring anyone back. 'Everyone was like, "Wow, look at this amazing thing," and I was like, "What the fuck are you guys talking about?", she said. 'We did the best we could, but on a totally real level we did nothing.' She added that she was aware she had 'a lot to say that could probably help people', but she was still dealing herself with the tangled grief about the incident. 'I have a lot that I still need to process myself and

will probably never be ready to talk about,' she acknowledged.

Ariana's willingness to be open with her emotions, both in the wake of the tragedy and in the years that followed, helped her fans. It modelled a healthy way of grappling with tragedy. She bravely stood up and didn't let hate win, which inspired everyone around her. 'Ariana's an open book,' Miley Cyrus told *Vogue* of her experience sharing the stage with Ariana at One Love Manchester. 'She has always shared her experiences with this beautiful blend of reality and the fantasy that pop culture requires. But holding her in my arms that night and feeling her shake from the loss of lives, literally feeling her heart pounding against mine – when you can let down the personas and cry with the rest of the world, it's unifying. It's a reminder that music can be our greatest healer.' Ariana, too, was healed by the music, both in performing it and in getting back into the studio. Fans waited patiently to see what she would do next and to learn how she would respond to the loss and the tragedy. Ariana would come back in the best way she knew how: with hope.

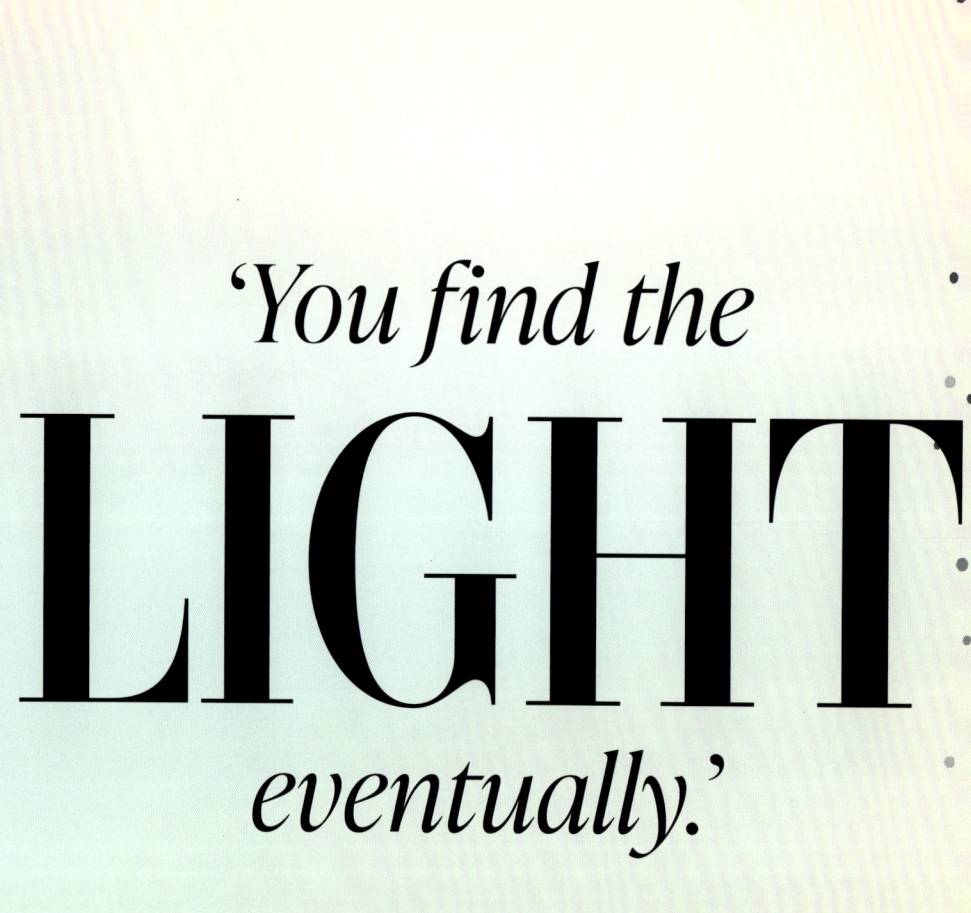

'You find the LIGHT eventually.'

4

The Light is
COMING

SWEETENER, THANK U, NEXT *and* COACHELLA

In the fog of grief, it can be difficult to see the other side, but from pain there is always an opportunity to heal. Although Ariana was only 23 years old when her concert in Manchester was bombed, she handled the tragedy with grace, wisdom and kindness, emphasizing that the quality of the response is always more important than the incident itself.

In her actions and her solidarity with fans, the singer affirmed that empathy outweighs hatred. She stood by her fans and she proved herself to be a person of true character. But in the months that followed the attack, and the eventual conclusion of her tour, Ariana was faced with yet another pivotal decision: how was she going to move forward from the darkness back into the light?

In typical fashion, shortly after completing *Dangerous Woman*, Ariana began working on her fourth album. In November 2016, she updated fans on Snapchat, confirming that she was already 'almost done with an album.' 'I didn't mean to make an album, and I don't know if it's done at all, but I just have a bunch of songs that I really like,' she clarified. 'I've just been working and creating and inspired.' Soon, though, Ariana was busy with the Dangerous Woman Tour and focused on her stage production. Then, Manchester happened. Ariana eventually resumed her tour and completed the scheduled dates, but it was uncertain when she might share new music. Her perspective on the world had been completely shattered, forcing her to re-establish what she believed in and how she wanted to express herself.

'I want it
to be

POSITIVE

and talk about
positivity and love.'

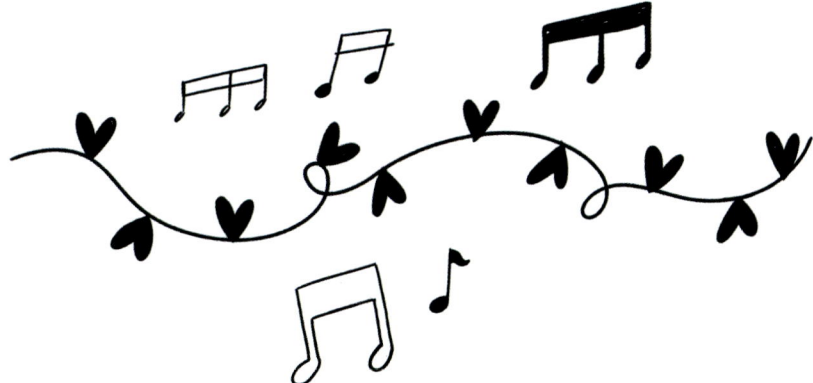

In September, as the Dangerous Woman Tour came to a close in Hong Kong, Ariana told *Billboard* that although the tour had been challenging she didn't want to just go home and relax. 'Knowing me, I'm going to be in the studio because I love it, and I want to create,' she said. 'I started an album already a year ago, over a year ago, but I want to keep creating, and it's not done yet. So I'm going to take my sweet ass time, so I'll be rested and ready to go again as soon as possible.' By December 2017, Ariana publicly began to tease an impending album, posting photos of her working in the studio on social media. On New Year's Eve, she posted a snippet of music on her Instagram page, captioning it, 'see u next year.'

But it would be several months before the singer actually revealed what she had been working on. She had a social-media hiatus and disappeared from view. It was the longest she had gone between releasing albums and anticipation built. Fans wondered if and how Ariana would address Manchester in her new music and whether her grief would impact her songwriting. She had established herself as a deft singer with a relatable approach to singing about relationships, both good and bad, but the fatal bombing was a far heavier subject to tackle than her relationships, particularly in pop music.

On 17 April 2018, Ariana announced a new single, 'No Tears Left to Cry.' She shared the news of the release, set for 20 April, on Twitter, adding, 'Missed you.' The song was written by Ariana and Savan Kotecha and co-written and produced by Max Martin and Ilya Salmanzadeh. It reflected Ariana's desire to say something uplifting following the events in Manchester. In the studio, she told Kotecha, 'I want it to be positive and talk about positivity and love. I don't have any tears left to cry.' 'We were like, that's it!' Kotecha recalled to *Billboard*. 'That's the way you say it!' There were many magical moments during the song's evolution. 'I feel like I watched this pop star turn into this true artist and her songwriting developed in extraordinary ways and it was a great experience,' he said. Ariana wanted the song to begin as a ballad, similar to Gloria Gaynor's hit 'I Will Survive,' and then for it to transform into something else. Frankie Grande recalled hearing an early version in the studio, noting, 'When I first heard it, they didn't have any lyrics. It was just the melody. They wrote the music first. The song really always had that sparkle.'

Ariana wrote 'No Tears Left to Cry' during the creation of her fourth album, which she eventually titled *Sweetener*. Her approached to the triumphant single came from a genuine

place of healing. 'When I started to take care of myself more, then came balance, and freedom, and joy,' she told *TIME*. 'It poured out into the music.' The song incorporated dance-pop, disco and R&B elements into its production. It was a celebratory, buoyant song, in both its melody and its lyrics. Its slow, emotional opening earned apt comparisons to Barbra Streisand and Donna Summer's 1979 song 'No More Tears (Enough Is Enough).' The song quickly shifted into something undeniable, with a beat suddenly dropping and propelling the melody forward. That aural shift was purposeful for the single's message. 'The intro is slow, and then it picks up,' Ariana explained to *TIME*. 'And it's about picking things up.'

Ariana and her songwriters kept the lyrical theme simple and sweet: in the wake of hardship, we can choose to change our mentality and to love, live and pick things up. It was emotional, despite Ariana's declaration of being done with tears, and it felt like a powerful catharsis, for the singer and for her fanbase. After the song was released, she thanked her listeners on Twitter. 'i have no idea where to start or what to say,' she wrote. 'i'm so unimaginably grateful for your love, warmth and kindness. i hope this song brings you light and comfort but also makes you wanna dance and live ya best life! i am so excited for this new chapter with you all. thank you for this beautiful start.'

The single received almost universal acclaim from critics. Not only was it a thoughtful response to a devastating tragedy, but it was also a genuinely good song. 'It's striking in its optimism: the soundtrack for the exact moment you decide to keep going,' *Pitchfork* wrote. *TIME* added, 'What happened

is part of the song, but the song is not about what happened. Instead of being elegiac, it's joyful and lush.' Much of the praise was directed at Ariana's ability to respond to terror with optimism. She could have released a sad song about a sorrowful moment, but instead, she chose to embody hope. She didn't want to exploit the memories of the fans who had died or the grief of those who had mourned them; she wanted to encourage joy.

In her *TIME* cover story, Ariana reflected on this decision, acknowledging that she understood the delicate balance between excavating the tragedy for art's sake and being disingenuous by turning it into pop music. 'Music is supposed to be the safest thing in the world,' she said. 'I think that's why it's still so heavy on my heart every single day.' Reflecting on the emotional fallout of the tragedy, she said that it felt like time was the only way she might find peace, adding, 'But every day I wait for that peace to come and it's still very painful.'

Ariana shared the music video for 'No Tears Left to Cry' on the same day she released the single. The video, directed by Dave Meyers, seemed visually to nod to Christopher Nolan's film *Inception* with its skewed cityscape. On a deeper level, though, it underscored the disorientation Ariana had felt and her struggle to regain solid footing. In one segment, she removed a mask of her face and

placed it alongside several others with varying expressions, an indication that she was unsure how best to present herself to the public. As Meyers explained in a behind-the-scenes clip, the video explored disorientation and what it feels like to 'find the ground again.' 'We sort of flirt with the ambiguity of whether you need to find the ground or whether the ground is what you make of it – sort of the optimism of the song and her, mixed with sort of the complexity and disillusionment of the world that we're putting her in.' At the end of the video, Ariana appeared in a field at sunrise with her dog Toulouse. A bee representing Manchester flew past the camera in a meaningful homage to the city.

'No Tears Left to Cry' debuted at No. 3 on the *Billboard* Hot 100 chart. It was hugely successful with fans and the song's music video eventually surpassed 1 billion views on YouTube. It was clear that listeners connected deeply with Ariana's strength and resilience and wanted to incorporate her anthem into their own lives. She performed the song live for the first time on the day of its release as a surprise guest during Kygo's set at Coachella. Several outlets had reported that Ariana might appear, but were uncertain with whom she would be collaborating. It was only hours after the single had dropped that she took to the stage on the Friday evening of the popular festival to showcase 'No Tears Left to Cry' and to perform a cover of Marvin Gaye's 1982 classic 'Sexual Healing'. She tinted her signature ponytail purple in honour of the occasion and paired it with a vibrant stage ensemble of the same shade. It was an epic comeback filled with welcome levity. Later, Ariana shared a photo of her hugging her boyfriend Mac Miller backstage and thanked Kygo for the opportunity. The single and the live performance opened a new chapter for Ariana, turning the page onto a promising future.

In early May, Ariana appeared on *The Tonight Show* and revealed that she planned to release her fourth album *Sweetener* later that summer. 'It's kind of about bringing light to a situation or to someone's life or somebody else brings life to your life,' she told host Jimmy Fallon. 'Sweetening the situation.' She also performed 'No Tears Left to Cry' live on TV for the first time on the late-night show, incorporating a set and background visuals that evoked the music video. Slowly, Ariana began to share more and more details about *Sweetener*, including that the album featured production from Pharrell Williams alongside Martin and Kotecha – her first time working directly with the musician and producer. Ariana told *TIME* that while she was in the studio with Williams 'there was nothing I wouldn't try'. She took the lead on the songwriting more than she had on prior albums and felt a newfound freedom to share her emotions, including her ongoing struggles with anxiety. 'I felt more inclined to tap into my feelings because I was spending more time with them,' she said. 'I was talking about them more. I was in therapy more.' She explained that she had 'never opened up' about her anxiety before, 'because I thought that was how life was supposed to feel.'

As Ariana re-emerged into the public sphere, her personal life was put back on display, too. She had been in a relationship with Miller since 2016, although she had been friends with the rapper since they were teenagers. They celebrated their romance on social media regularly and were often photographed together. He had been there for her in the aftermath of Manchester and had supported her as she worked on new music. But in May, shortly after announcing *Sweetener*, Ariana and Miller confirmed they had amicably parted ways as girlfriend and boyfriend. Ariana shared a photo of the couple on Instagram, writing, 'I respect and adore him endlessly and am grateful to have him in my life in any form, at all times, regardless of how our relationship changes or what the universe holds for each of us!' She added, 'Unconditional love is not selfish. It is wanting the best for someone even if at the moment, it's not you.'

Shortly after the breakup, Ariana began dating comedian and *Saturday Night Live* cast member Pete Davidson. Fans speculated loudly about when the relationship had begun and worried that her breakup with Miller had negatively impacted the rapper's mental health. Not long after Ariana's relationship with Davidson became public, Miller was arrested for driving drunk in the San Fernando Valley outside Los Angeles. He crashed his Mercedes-Benz G-Wagon into a pole and knocked it down, before fleeing the scene on foot. One of Miller's fans publicly blamed Ariana online for the incident. Ariana couldn't hold her tongue and in a social media post, she described her partnership with Miller as 'toxic'. 'I have cared for him and tried to support his sobriety for years (and always will of course),' she wrote. 'But shaming/blaming women for a man's inability to

'It's kind of
about bringing

LIGHT,

to a

situation...'

keep his shit together is a very major problem. Let's please stop doing that.' The fan apologized. Ariana's response helped to silence the criticism and she tried to move forward as best she could. She and Davidson continued to share their relationship online, including revealing their matching tattoos, and by mid-June Davidson confirmed that the couple was engaged.

As the tabloids grew increasingly obsessed with her personal life, Ariana announced a pre-order for *Sweetener* and released a promotional single, 'The Light Is Coming', which featured Nicki Minaj. Ariana co-wrote the song with Williams, while Minaj penned her own verse, which opened the track. Notably, 'The Light Is Coming' sampled an audio clip from

news channel CNN of a man named Craig Miller shouting at former US Senator Arlen Specter during a town-hall meeting in Pennsylvania in 2009, accusing him of not letting anyone else speak. The thudding, dance-ready single was more stripped back than 'No Tears Left to Cry', although it similarly emphasized focusing on the light over the dark. It earned mixed reviews; critics praised the hypnotic production and experimental approach to pop music, but some were unconvinced by the overall result. *SPIN* called it 'a Frankensteinian product that Ariana makes all her own', while *Rolling Stone* described the song as 'a weak spot: a fun beat swallowed by the repetition of an unnecessary, overly prominent' sample.

But Ariana had barely scratched the surface of *Sweetener*. In July, she shared the album's second official single, a powerful pop anthem titled 'God Is a Woman'. The song represented another collaboration between Ariana, Martin, Kotecha and Salmanzadeh, this time with the help of songwriter Rickard Göransson. A version of it had originally been written for Camila Cabello. But as Cabello acknowledged on SiriusXM's *Radio Andy* in 2019, 'It didn't end up sounding right for me'. The songwriters considered taking it to a rapper next. As Kotecha told *Billboard*, who else 'would be able to say and carry a full song about saying God is a woman?' Salmanzadeh, who also produced the single, suggested they offer it to Ariana. 'We played it for her and she just lost her shit,'

Kotecha said. 'She said, "That's not for a rapper, that's mine, I'm taking that."' Ariana returned the next day with lyrics she had written and they finished the song. 'When she started laying down "God Is a Woman", it all became alive,' Kotecha said. 'Sometimes, the right idea has to find the right home, and it found the right home.' Before hearing the song, Ariana thought *Sweetener* was done, but she ultimately recorded it two days before the meeting with her record label to play them the album for the first time – an impactful last-minute addition.

The mid-tempo single combined pop and R&B influences, with Ariana's vocals layered numerous times to create the effect of a choir. It saw Ariana taking a defiant, feminist stand against her critics as she also asserted her

sexuality. She was flourishing, she insisted in the lyrics, no matter how often people came for her. The potentially controversial title wasn't intended to be taken literally; it was a symbolic representation of a woman embodying her power without hesitation. The music video, again directed by Meyers, augmented that message with a series of impactful visuals, including Ariana floating naked in a vagina-shaped pool of colourful liquid and Ariana sitting on top of a giant book as men hurled stereotypical misogynistic insults at her. In a particularly jarring moment, stop-motion gophers emerged from a desiccated landscape and screamed. 'That feels like how I feel at times being a woman who is misunderstood and constantly labelled or pinned down as one thing or another,' Ariana explained of the animals on the *Zach Sang Show*. She added that being so misunderstood sometimes made her want to scream. 'Like, "Hi, I'm not just a vagina,"' she said. 'We've been screaming for decades for equality and also to be understood and to feel heard. To be seen also as not just a vessel for sex. Which we totally can be if we choose to be also.'

Midway through the song's music video, Ariana turned to the camera and lip-synced to a voice recording of Madonna reciting a version of Bible verse Ezekiel 25:17, in homage to *Pulp Fiction*. The iconic pop star lent her voice to the video as a favour to Ariana. 'I texted her because without Madonna I wouldn't be able to make a song like that,' Ariana recounted on *The Tonight Show*. 'She paved the way for all of us, and has been here fighting that fight way longer than any of us. Of course I immediately thought of her to be involved somehow because without her I wouldn't be able to make that song.' Madonna recorded seven takes of the part at a studio in Portugal where she was working. On the *Zach Sang Show* Ariana shared that Madonna told her the video treatment was 'risqué' and that she was 'very proud.' 'It was really surreal and I sent her the final product and I remember she said – I could literally cry – "I'm so proud of you. Keep fighting the fight."'

Ariana released *Sweetener* on 17 August 2018, more than two years after *Dangerous Woman*. She described the album as showcasing a 'sweeter, more mature side of my voice' and said it used 'newer parts' of her vocal range. Although she had written most of it while in a relationship with Miller, she added a song about her new beau, titled 'Pete Davidson', towards the end of the production. Ariana wrote the short, intimate interlude track with Monét and producers Tommy Brown and Charles Anderson. It lasted less than two minutes, but featured Ariana confidently calling Davidson her 'soulmate' and affirming how happy he made her. Not all of her fans appreciated the song, but Ariana wasn't standing for any more criticism and defended herself on Twitter: 'I been the fuck thru it and life's too short to be cryptic n shit about something as beautiful as this love I'm in.'

The album's closing track 'Get Well Soon' was written with Williams as a way to address what had happened in Manchester more directly than 'No Tears Left to Cry.' The song layered Ariana's voice on top of itself for emotional effect. 'It's all the voices in my head talking to one another,' Ariana explained to *ELLE*. At the end of the song, she included 40 seconds of silence in homage to the victims. In total, the track clocked in at 5:22, the date of the bombing. The singer told *Paper* that Williams 'forced it out of me' while she was in a negative mental space. 'I've always had anxiety,

I've had anxiety for years,' she explained. 'But when I got home from tour it reached a very different, intense peak. It became physical and I was not going out at all, and I felt like I was outside my body.' She had experienced something like déjà vu, she said, 'but like 24/7 for three months at a time.' She explained, '[Pharrell] was like, "You have to write about it. You need to make this into music and get this shit out, and I promise it will heal you." And it definitely helped.' She added that 'Get Well Soon' felt like 'one of the most important songs I'll ever write.'

Sweetener represented an upswing in Ariana's life and career. She had stepped into a new, defining chapter and her fans were responding positively. She was happy, as she repeatedly shared in interviews about the album. Her positive attitude was so infectious that it made her mom cry every time they spoke on FaceTime. 'I feel very open and honest and chill,' she said on the *Zach Sang Show*. 'I feel like myself again.' She added of the source of her happiness, 'I think it's just where I'm at. It's a combination of everything.' But for every upswing there is an inevitable downfall. At 25 years old, Ariana had already experienced more than her share of hardship. She had faced real tragedy and overcome it. But life is never fair, even for famous pop stars.

On 7 September 2018, police officers responded to an emergency 911 call from Miller's personal assistant and sober coach. When they arrived at the rapper's house, the officers found Miller's lifeless body in a bedroom. He was 26 years old. It was later confirmed that Miller, a longtime addict, had died of an accidental overdose. An autopsy found fentanyl, cocaine and alcohol in his system, despite his many attempts to get

sober. He had recently released a new album, *Swimming*, which reflected on his breakup with Ariana in many of the songs. His death shook Ariana to her core. She stayed silent for several days, grieving privately. Her friends, including Victoria Monét and her childhood pal Aaron Gross, gathered around her. A week after his death, Ariana shared a thoughtful tribute to Miller, her friend and former boyfriend. 'i adored you from the day i met you when i was nineteen and i always will,' she wrote on Instagram. 'i can't believe you aren't here anymore. i really can't wrap my head around it. we talked about this. so many times. i'm so mad, i'm so sad i don't know what to do. you were my dearest friend. for so long. above anything else. i'm so sorry i couldn't fix or take your pain away. i really wanted to. the kindest, sweetest soul with demons he never deserved. i hope you're okay now. rest.'

Later, Ariana opened up more about having spent years trying to help Miller with his sobriety. She supported him first as a friend, then as his girlfriend. But as anyone who loves an addict knows, it is impossible to fix the underlying problem from the outside. She recalled worrying about him constantly. While on the Dangerous Woman Tour, Ariana stayed up late at night, obsessing about whether he was safe. She described her grief over his death as 'pretty all-consuming.' 'He was the best person ever, and he didn't deserve the demons he had,' she told *Vogue*. 'I was the glue for such a long time, and I found myself becoming less and less sticky. The pieces just started to float away.'

The month following Miller's death, after a lot of tabloid drama, Ariana and Davidson called off their engagement. Ariana didn't address the split right away, but she did

'I don't remember those MONTHS of my life because I was a) so drunk and b) so sad.'

reference it cryptically on social media. After filming NBC's *A Very Wicked Halloween* in October 2018, she posted on Instagram, 'Ok today was v special and I'm so grateful I was able to be there. Time to say bye bye to the internet for just a lil bit.' She added, 'Its very sad and were all tryin very hard to keep goin.' Unsurprisingly, Ariana dealt with her overwhelming heartbreak through music. She released a new single, 'Thank U, Next', on 3 November 2018. The lyrics referenced several of her exes, including Davidson, Big Sean, Ricky Alvarez and Miller, although she began writing it while still together with Davidson. She revealed on the *Zach Sang Show* that she actually recorded three version of the song. 'In my relationship at the time, things were like up and down and on and off, and so I didn't know what was going to happen and then we got back together,' she said. 'So I had to make a different version of it, and then we broke up again, so we ended up going with that verse.'

While Ariana had survived breakups before (and would again), she admitted to feeling a deep sadness that her short-lived relationship with Davidson had ended. 'remember when i was like hey i have no tears left to cry and the universe was like HAAAAAAAAA bitch u thought,' she wrote on Twitter. She had thought she was healed, at least partially, after Manchester, as reflected by the songs on *Sweetener*. But Ariana wasn't okay. Not after Manchester, not after Miller's death, not after her breakup with Davidson. Her friends urged her to put that sadness into making more music. So, she wrote and recorded and forced herself to face the lingering demons and the unshakeable grief, and soon she had a new album, *Thank U, Next*.

'If I'm completely honest, I don't remember those months of my life because I was a) so drunk and b) so sad,' she told *Vogue*. 'I don't really remember how it started or how it finished, or how all of a sudden there were ten songs on the board.'

Thank U, Next, a collaboration with several producers, including Martin and Salmanzadeh, reckoned with Ariana's life up to this point. The single 'Thank U, Next' focused on her past relationships, acknowledging the positives and negatives of each, but ultimately the album was about Ariana and her identity. 'I think that this is the first album and also the first year of my life where I'm realizing that I can no longer put off spending time with myself, just as me,' she explained to *Vogue*. 'I've been boo'd up my entire adult life. I've always had someone to say goodnight to. So *Thank U, Next* was this moment of self-realization. It was this scary moment of "Wow, you have to face all this stuff now. No more distractions. You have to heal all this shit."'

Even compared with her prior albums, *Thank U, Next* was written and recorded quickly. Ariana told Zach Sang that the experience 'kind of saved my life.' 'I don't think life has ever been as bad as it was when [we started],' she admitted. Monét was an essential collaborator, co-writing six of the album's tracks. 'It goes without saying that it was a very trying time, but music naturally is a healing mechanism,' Monét told *Rolling Stone*. 'That's what we were holding on to – along with some champagne glasses.' Notably, nine of the LP's twelve songs had two or more female writers, a first on one of Ariana's albums. Ariana told *Billboard* the album was the result of 'feminine energy and champagne and music and laughter and crying.'

Ariana shared two more singles, '7 Rings' and 'Break Up with Your Girlfriend, I'm Bored', before the album officially arrived on 8 February 2019. '7 Rings', a chart-topping hit from the get-go, centred on an interpolation of showtune 'My Favorite Things' from *The Sound of Music*. The hip-hop-inspired pop song came out of a 'challenging fall day' Ariana had while in New York City making the album. 'Me and my friends went to Tiffany's together, just because we needed some retail therapy,' she recounted in an interview with *Billboard*. 'You know how when you're waiting at Tiffany's they give you lots of champagne? They got us very tipsy, so we bought seven engagement rings, and when I got back to the studio I gave everybody a friendship ring.' The track reclaimed Ariana's happiness, with the lyrics admitting that she should be a 'sad girl' based

on everything that had happened. But she refused to succumb to that sadness, even if it meant indulging in something as shallow as retail therapy, and urged the listener to seek solace from their friends instead of from a romantic relationship.

'Break Up with Your Girlfriend, I'm Bored' was less of an emotional release. It featured an interpolation of NSYNC's song 'It Makes Me Ill' and replaced a song called 'Remember' on the album's set list. Ariana explained to fans on Twitter that she made the swap to support her mental health, not because she was afraid to share the original track. 'I just want to feel stable and ok sharing, promoting, performing the songs for u which I wouldn't,' she wrote. 'I decided to keep it private for many reasons.' 'Break Up with Your Girlfriend, I'm Bored', a mid-tempo R&B pop number, saw Ariana

WITH PETE DAVIDSON

encouraging a man to leave his significant other for her. Its music video, directed by Hannah Lux Davis, mirrored the lyrics, with actor Charles Melton and model Ariel Yasmine playing the central couple. Instead of luring Melton's character away from his girlfriend, however, the video ended with a surprise twist as Ariana and Yasmine kissed. Critics described the clip as 'sexy and stylish' and compared it to the thriller film *Single White Female*, although some outlets and fans accused Ariana of queer-baiting because she was a straight woman. However, because Yasmine's character looked so much like Ariana herself, others suggested that perhaps the message was about self-love, rather than sexuality – an idea that resonated with the album's overall theme.

In the fall of 2018, Ariana announced her fourth global tour, the Sweetener World Tour.

She had been hinting at a return to the road for a while and she had done a series of promotional shows, the Sweetener Sessions, around the release of the album. But fans were eagerly awaiting a proper follow-up to the Dangerous Woman Tour. This tour would promote two albums at once, something that Ariana told *Billboard* in 2018 was a goal of hers. 'I don't want to do what people tell me to do, I don't want to conform to the pop star agenda,' she said. 'I want to do it on my own terms from now on. If I want to tour two albums at once, I'm going to tour two albums at once.' She added that she was focused on doing what was 'authentic and honest and natural' to her. 'It's the only way that I've been able to survive,' she said.

The demand for tickets was intense. After sharing the initial tour dates, Ariana quickly

added more shows, both in North America and Europe, as earlier ones sold out. The singer decided to partner with nonprofit voter-registration group HeadCount for the tour to help register new US voters ahead of the 2020 Presidential Election, eventually registering a record-breaking 33,381 new voters. 'I'm so incredibly proud of my fans for engaging in this,' Ariana acknowledged on Twitter when the number was revealed. 'thank u so much for investing in our future and for committing to making a change together.'

To design the tour, Ariana enlisted Brian and Scott Nicholson (known as The Twins) as its creative directors, LeRoy Bennett as the production designer and Jason Baeri as the lighting director. The aesthetic centred on an orb shape and the intention was to create an ethereal vibe. 'She's very into the cosmos and the spirituality of all of that and the feminism of a sphere,' Bennett told *The Hollywood Reporter*. 'It's not hard, it's not sharp; it's soft and round and beautiful. That's kind of the branding of the tour and what's going on with her at the moment.' He also explained that the tour's lighting was unconventional for a pop star. 'Normally most artists are lit like colour-corrected white spots and stand out a lot more than anybody else,' Bennett noted. 'Where in Ariana's case, she's part of the environment.' The tour featured numerous costume changes with the singer again styled by Law Roach, who incorporated bright colours such as lavender and orange into her costumes and accessories. Many of the custom outfits, created by designers such as Michael Ngo and Unravel, were two-piece ensembles with matching boots, intended to highlight her movement on stage.

The overall result was dramatic and immersive, with nods to Ariana's past, present and future throughout. As many fans noted on the tour's opening night in Albany, New York, she paid subtle tribute to Miller by playing his music in the venue before taking the stage. It marked her biggest tour to date, and it was bolstered by the success of her recent albums and her omnipresent status in the media. *Rolling Stone* described the show as a 'victory lap' and a 'proof of life.' 'If Grande wanted to sit this touring cycle out, her fans probably would've understood,' the publication wrote in a review of the first performance. 'But she chose not to, and that speaks volumes to the strength she's built this show around.' *The Telegraph* called it 'a night of magic and melancholy from the most exciting young star in pop.' Ariana performed ten concerts on the initial North American leg before taking a short pause to fulfil a bucket-list dream: headlining Coachella.

Although Ariana had taken the stage at Coachella the year before, her two headlining performances at the music festival in April 2019 marked a groundbreaking, historical moment. In January, she was announced as one of the three headlining acts, alongside Childish Gambino and Tame Impala. At 25 years old, she became the youngest performer to ever headline the two-weekend event. In addition, she was only the fourth female artist to take a top slot on the bill, following Beyoncé, Lady Gaga and Björk. 'humbled and excited as all hell,' Ariana tweeted when the lineup was announced. Fans anticipated the moment with typical fervour, dubbing it 'Arichella' in honour of the singer. The performance was ostensibly part of her Sweetener World Tour, but Ariana wanted to involve special guests and bring something different to the audience.

their 1997 hit 'Tearin' Up My Heart', filling in on vocals for absent band member Justin Timberlake. It made for a memorable pop-culture moment as Ariana performed the song's iconic dance moves alongside the band. When the band exited the stage, she sighed with happiness, saying, 'I could die now.' Minaj later joined her for their two collaborations, 'Side To Side' and 'Bang Bang', while Ariana tapped Diddy and Mase for a rendition of Notorious B.I.G.'s 'Mo Money Mo Problems'. The set culminated with 'No Tears Left to Cry' and 'Thank U, Next', performed to the explosion of fireworks around the stage.

The critical response to Ariana's performance was particularly laudatory, despite a few technical issues Minaj experienced on stage. *NME* described it as 'virtually flawless', noting that the set featured 'surprises and throwbacks, fireworks and costume changes, and some very slick, very aesthetically pleasing production.' *The Guardian* remarked that the 25-song performance was emblematic of Ariana's work to date. 'Her work forms a fascinating, still-unfolding pop Bildungsroman: every sexual epiphany and personal milestone sketched out in real time,' the newspaper wrote. 'You can see why she is such an icon to a generation who also tell their own stories in public, via Snapchat and Instagram.'

Ariana repeated the triumphant set again the following weekend, providing an uplifting conclusion to the music festival. Minaj and NSYNC didn't return, but Bieber made a surprise appearance to duet with Ariana on his song 'Sorry'. 'This is my first time performing here in two years, and I had to get my groove back, get my swag back, you know what I'm saying,' Bieber told the audience, confirming

On the Sunday evening of the festival's first weekend, Ariana opened her set with a dynamic rendition of 'God Is a Woman'. Her enthusiasm and excitement were apparent, particularly as she introduced a variety of guests throughout the lengthy set, including NSYNC, Nicki Minaj, and Diddy and Mase. NSYNC's Lance Bass, Joey Fatone, Chris Kirkpatrick and JC Chasez emerged early on in the performance to help Ariana showcase 'Break Up With Your Girlfriend, I'm Bored'. 'Coachella, I've been rehearsing my whole motherfucking life for this moment,' Ariana acknowledged before joining the singers for

'I have to be
the luckiest
GIRL
in the world, and
the unluckiest,
for sure.'

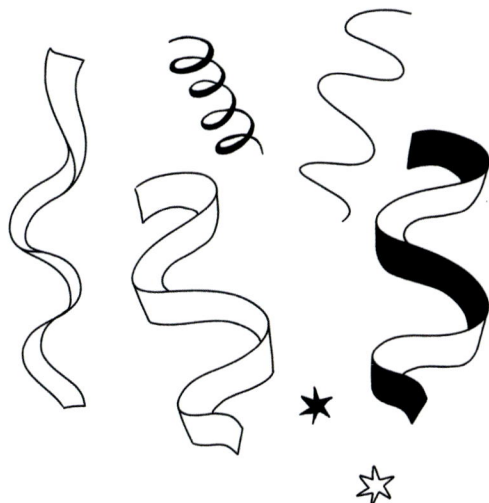

that the performance had come about at the very last second. To encourage the crowd, he added, 'She's amazing, give her more energy!' The lack of special guests didn't deter Ariana. In fact, putting herself in the spotlight for more of the set seemed to enliven fans and critics. 'It's clear now that Ariana, the youngest performer ever to headline Coachella at age 25, didn't need the security blanket of special guests or gimmicks,' Palm Springs' *Desert Sun* wrote. 'Instead her voice starred.'

Within days of Coachella, Ariana was back on the road for the Sweetener World Tour. She performed dozens of shows throughout the spring and summer and headlined Lollapalooza in Chicago, Illinois before flying to London in mid-August to kick off the European leg with three nights at the O2 Arena. The tour returned to North America in November, where it concluded in Inglewood, California on 22 December 2019. Ariana ultimately played 97 concerts over the course of the year, performing for more than 1.3 million fans. It became her highest-grossing tour to date, a significant achievement after so many ups and downs.

As the tour wound to a close, Ariana dabbled in a few other musical endeavours.

She was co-executive producer, alongside Kotecha, of the soundtrack for the film reboot of *Charlie's Angels*, and contributed several songs, including girl-power anthem 'Don't Call Me Angel', a collaboration with Miley Cyrus and Lana Del Rey. She joined Lizzo on a remix of the singer's hit song 'Good as Hell', for which Ariana penned a new verse. By the end of the year, accolades had poured in. Spotify revealed Ariana as the fourth most-streamed artist of the 2010s and the third most-streamed artist of 2019. *NME* named her one of the ten musical artists who defined the decade, writing that 'she exits the 2010s one of the most successful, impressive and resilient musicians on the planet.' *Thank U, Next* became the eighth-bestselling album of 2019 globally.

There was no denying what Ariana had overcome to get here. She had become an undeniable force despite a series of tragedies and heartbreaks. 'I have to be the luckiest girl in the world, and the unluckiest, for sure,' Ariana told *Vogue*. 'I'm walking this fine line between healing myself and not letting the things that I've gone through be picked at before I'm ready.' As the decade neared its end, more challenges were looming. But so were opportunities for Ariana to prove herself worthy once again.

5

Yes, AND?

POSITIONS, COLLABORATIONS *and ETERNAL* SUNSHINE

In early 2020, a mysterious illness began circulating the globe, first in China and then onward to the US. The virus, eventually named COVID-19, was contagious and deadly, and most governments struggled to know how to respond properly. A pandemic was unprecedented in modern times and it effectively paused the lives of everyone who wasn't an essential worker, a sudden shift that isolated people from friends, family and their jobs. Performers who made much of their living on the road saw their careers come to a complete standstill. After a world tour, two successful albums and numerous awards show appearances, the most recent of which was a spectacular four-song performance at the 62nd annual Grammys in late January (images that lingered with fans after lockdown hit), Ariana found herself trapped at home along with the rest of the world.

By mid-March, much of the United States had shut down. People waited with anxious anticipation to see how long the situation would last. Ariana, at home in Los Angeles, did the best she could under the circumstances. She spoke out on social media in favour of social distancing and safety. 'Please don't turn

a blind eye,' she wrote on Instagram. 'It is incredibly dangerous and selfish to take this situation that lightly. The "We will be fine because we're young" mindset is putting people who aren't young and/or healthy in a lot of danger. You sound stupid and privileged and you need to care more about others.' The singer shared a list of helpful organizations, encouraging her online audience to donate to those in greater need. 'While we are social distancing and doing the best we can to protect one another, my heart hurts for the small businesses, individuals, and families affected by all of this,' she wrote. In the weeks that followed, numerous fans came forward to say that Ariana had sent them money using the payment app Venmo to help with their bills. 'She reached out and took care of my salary for the month,' one fan told *The New York Post*.

It quickly became clear the pandemic would last longer than a few weeks. It wasn't a temporary situation and wouldn't simply vanish. A new normal began to solidify. Musicians and actors collaborated virtually and live-streamed at-home performances, often to benefit particular charities. Online engagement was at an all-time high. Fans gravitated towards anything that felt like a respite from the dire news cycle. Everyone was looking for fleeting connection amid forced isolation, and new music was sparse. So, when Ariana and Justin Bieber announced a joint single, 'Stuck With U', in late April, fans exhaled a sigh of collective relief. It reminded people that there was still the possibility for something new and that artists could make things together, albeit remotely. The pop song was co-written by Gian Stone, Skyler Stonestreet, Freddy Wexler and Whitney

Phillips. They initially sent the track to Ariana's team, imagining it as a solo single. Ariana recorded a version that same night in her home studio and suggested it would sound even better with an added male vocalist. She asked the writers if she could send it to Bieber, who was an ideal fit since they shared a manager. 'The stars really aligned,' Stone said later of the track. The musicians announced that all net proceeds from 'Stuck With U' would be donated to the First Responders Children's Foundation to provide scholarships to children of frontline workers whose lives were impacted by the pandemic, which was in part why Ariana had agreed to release it. She told Zane Lowe on Apple Music that her intention was to help fans through the difficult time, not simply to publicize new material. 'We wanted to put music out because music is the thing that makes people feel good,' she said.

'It's the thing that speaks most to people's spirits, and we just wanted to lift them.'

On the surface, 'Stuck With U' seemed to be a reflection on the lockdown. Its title and lyrics referenced a couple who were literally stuck inside together, but the song was about something more universal and timeless. Ariana and Bieber sang about what it feels like to want to stay with someone for a lifetime. Why go outside, the song asked, when you have everything you need right here? It was a fitting sentiment for the moment, connecting with fans on a literal level, but it also exemplified the bigger relationship themes that both artists have historically favoured in their work. Scooter Braun, Ariana and Bieber's manager and a co-writer on the track, called the song 'The duet for our times' in a tweet prior to its release.

Because Ariana and Bieber couldn't shoot a music video in person, they created one tailored to the isolated circumstances of the pandemic. Ariana and Bieber shot their own segments and intercut them with videos submitted by young fans who were stuck at home. 'I want to see you guys having fun in quarantine,' Bieber wrote in a call for submissions. 'This is the prom song for everyone who can't go to prom now.' It featured cameos from Demi Lovato, Elizabeth Gillies, Gwyneth Paltrow, Hailey Baldwin, Paula Abdul, Ayesha and Steph Curry, Kendall and Kylie Jenner, 2 Chainz, and Ashton Kutcher and Mila Kunis. At the end of the music video, Ariana could be seen embracing Dalton Gomez, a real-estate agent who eventually became her husband (and, later, her ex-husband) – a cheeky surprise for fans. A few days after the video dropped on 8 May, Bieber shared a second 'Mother's Day' edition of the video, featuring video clips of fans with their moms.

A week after its release, 'Stuck With U' debuted at No. 1 on the *Billboard* Hot 100 chart, marking Ariana's third No. 1 single and Bieber's sixth. It became remarkably successful, bolstered by the dearth of new music, and the song was embraced by fans around the world. But the release was not without its controversy. After the first-week chart emerged, rapper Tekashi69 accused Ariana and Bieber of buying their No. 1 spot. 'I want the world to know that *Billboard* is a lie,' he said in a video to fans. 'You can buy No. 1s on *Billboard*.' The rapper suggested that Ariana's team had purchased 60,000 units of the song using six different credit cards, leading her to respond in

WITH CHRISSY TEIGEN AT THE JANUARY 2020 62ND ANNUAL GRAMMY AWARDS

her defence. In a brutally honest Instagram post, Ariana made clear that 'numbers aren't the driving force' for her and that it was her fans who had generated the song's rapid success. 'U can not discredit this as hard as u try', she wrote. 'To anybody that is displeased with their placement on the chart this week or who is spending their time racking their brain thinking of as many ways as they can to discredit hardworking women (and only the women for some reason...), i ask u to take a moment to humble yourself'. *Billboard* also published a response, explaining how the publication calculated the charts and refuting all of Tekashi69's claims. Ariana had earned the accolade on her own merit.

Meanwhile, Ariana continued writing music by herself. She worked throughout lockdown, but told Lowe that she didn't 'really feel comfortable' releasing anything beyond 'Stuck With U' while the global circumstances were so calamitous. The isolation bolstered her artistic output, even if she wasn't yet in a position to share it. 'It's a great time to create because you're stuck with your thoughts and left in your head a little bit, so I think all creatives are extra inspired right now', she

told Lowe. Having a home-studio setup had been fun, but it was detrimental to her eating and sleeping routine. 'I have to remember that there is life outside of making stuff and I have to leave the computer at some point', she said. 'I think as far as creating goes, it feels really good'.

Soon after 'Stuck With U' dropped, Ariana was part of another collaboration. She appeared as a guest vocalist on Lady Gaga's single 'Rain on Me', from the pop star's forthcoming LP *Chromatica*, although the track was technically created before COVID-19 hit. The single arrived on 22 May 2020 alongside a futuristic music video from director Robert Rodriguez, shot prior to the pandemic, and the two musicians shared a skit they filmed for *The Weather Channel* in their respective Los Angeles homes to promote the song. The empowering track saw the pair performing a dynamic duet over a euphoric beat. The lyrics emphasized an eventual triumph no matter the weather. It was a remarkable two-hander, resulting in rave reviews and a No. 1 debut on the *Billboard* Hot 100 chart. Speaking to Lowe, Lady Gaga explained that recording the song had been

'It's a great time to **CREATE** because you're stuck with your thoughts and left in your head a little bit...'

'I know
that in my

HEART

this will make a
lot of people feel
something good.'

a 'very healing process for me' because she'd been able to impart her wisdom on Ariana after 'not necessarily having a female artist that mentored me as I came up.' Lady Gaga shared that she'd told the younger singer, 'Anything that you feel chains you, any pop cultural construct that you feel you have to live up to, I'd ask you to please forget about it and be yourself.'

On 30 August 2020, as COVID-19 restrictions slowly eased, Ariana teamed up with Lady Gaga to perform 'Rain on Me' live at the 2020 MTV Video Music Awards. The track was up for seven awards: Song of the Year, Video of the Year, Best Collaboration, Best Pop, Best Cinematography, Best Choreography and Best Visual Effects, eventually winning Song of the Year, Best Collaboration and Best Cinematography. For the performance, Lady Gaga took the stage to showcase a medley of songs from *Chromatica* wearing a high-tech mask. Ariana, also masked, joined midway through, with the pair reviving the impressive choreography from their music video. During a period of isolation and uncertainty, the joyous performance offered a much-needed sense of uplift for viewers, a reminder that we could still be together as long as we stayed safe.

As time passed, people became more accustomed to the new world order. Musicians made albums virtually or recorded together in bubbles. Touring still didn't seem possible, but things couldn't stay on pause forever; artists had to find a way to move forward. Although Ariana had confirmed in April that she was writing and recording new material at home, there had been no sense of whether she actually planned to release a follow-up to *Thank U, Next* anytime soon. Then, on 14 October 2020, Ariana tweeted 'i can't wait to give u my album this month.' Three days later, she announced its title, *Positions*, and launched a countdown clock on her website ticking down to 23 October, when she shared the album's debut single, also called 'Positions.'

Despite having her new album ready, Ariana wasn't sure whether this was an appropriate time to unveil it. Ultimately, she decided it was more important to gift her fans something that would make them smile than to overthink the timing. 'I've seen them on the timeline worried about their lives and the state of the world all year,' she explained in an interview on the *Zach Sang Show*. 'I know that in my heart this will make a lot of people feel something good.' She added that the galvanizing response to her album announcement underscored why that felt so right. 'I had chills,' she admitted. 'It's a really terrifying, but also beautiful thing.'

Along with the single, Ariana released a cinematic music video for 'Positions', directed by Dave Meyers. It showed Ariana taking over the top role in the White House with characteristic immaculate style. The single, produced by London on da Track, Tommy Brown and Mr. Franks, embraced Ariana's signature blend of airy pop and melodic R&B. She sang about her dedication to a lover and her willingness to get down and dirty, in the kitchen or in the bedroom. It had a breezy pop hook, with an immediately catchy chorus, and felt effervescent and confident – an ideal aural aesthetic coming out of lockdown. The lyrics cheekily acknowledged that women can be more than one thing and were sweetly provocative without an overuse of innuendo: a fun-loving song about intimacy with a memorable partner. The single heralded the album itself, offering a glimpse of the singer's intention to remain true to her aesthetic core rather than completely reinvent her style.

Thanks to her steadfast approach, 'Positions' debuted at No. 1 on the *Billboard* Hot 100 chart, extending Ariana's record for the most No. 1 debuts in history, with five top-charting singles to date. Grande also became the first artist to have the most singles debut at No. 1 in a single calendar year after the incredible success of 'Stuck with U' and 'Rain on Me.'

Positions, Ariana's sixth studio album, arrived on 30 October, with '34+35' as the second single. The LP featured collaborations with multiple producers, including Brown, and several co-writers, notably her longtime writing partners and old friends Victoria Monét and Tayla Parx. She tapped fellow artists Doja Cat, The Weeknd and Ty Dolla $ign for vocal features. Ariana explained that her intention with the album was to 'continue the story' she'd been telling with her previous projects, but also, she revealed to Zach Sang, to 'sing a little more.' The songs represented a new chapter for the singer, who described *Positions* as coming from a 'more healed place' than *Thank U, Next*.

Sonically, Ariana incorporated a broader range of vocals, string instrumentation and sophisticated orchestration alongside the wry lyrics. It adhered to Ariana's love for pop and R&B while also drawing inspiration from multiple other genres, such as funk and disco. It felt flirtatious and buoyant, much like 'Positions', although some critics commented on a notable lack of evolution within the music – a sentiment that was not always a bad thing. 'Many pop stars attempt to take their sound to the next level by making increasingly grand and bombastic big-tent statements,' *The New*

York Times noted. 'Grande has succeeded largely by doing just the opposite: turning her music into an atmosphere as intimate as her bedroom, a place where she's sometimes entertaining a lover but just as often cracking goofy jokes with her closest friends.'

Ariana had hinted at 'Motive', a collaboration with Doja Cat, months earlier. The duo began writing the song, originally titled 'Motivate', in 2019, after Ariana sent Doja Cat the idea. Doja Cat loved the song so much she sent Ariana a video the next morning. In the clip, she twerked so hard her wig flew off. The singer already had her whole verse ready to go. 'I was like, "Take as many bars as you want. Do it. If you're inspired to say stuff, let's go,"' Ariana told Zane Lowe. 'And so she just goes off on it, and it's so much fun, and I love it. It's my favourite so far.' The thumping dance-pop song, produced by Murda Beatz and Brown, saw the singers guessing what a potential partner might want.

Although 'Off the Table', a vulnerable R&B ballad, was released as one of the album's singles, Ariana admitted she had been initially unsure whether she would share it with the public. One of her producers, Shintaro, sent her a collection of beats and she wrote a verse and a chorus to one of them. After she sent it to The Weeknd, he immediately replied that he would write the second verse. 'It was a very intimate moment and writing process between two friends,' Ariana said on the *Zach Sang Show*. The song came from a deeply emotional place, asking whether love can be possible again after going through something traumatic. Fans have long speculated that it is about her relationship with Mac Miller and her subsequent short-lived engagement to Pete Davidson – details she herself has never

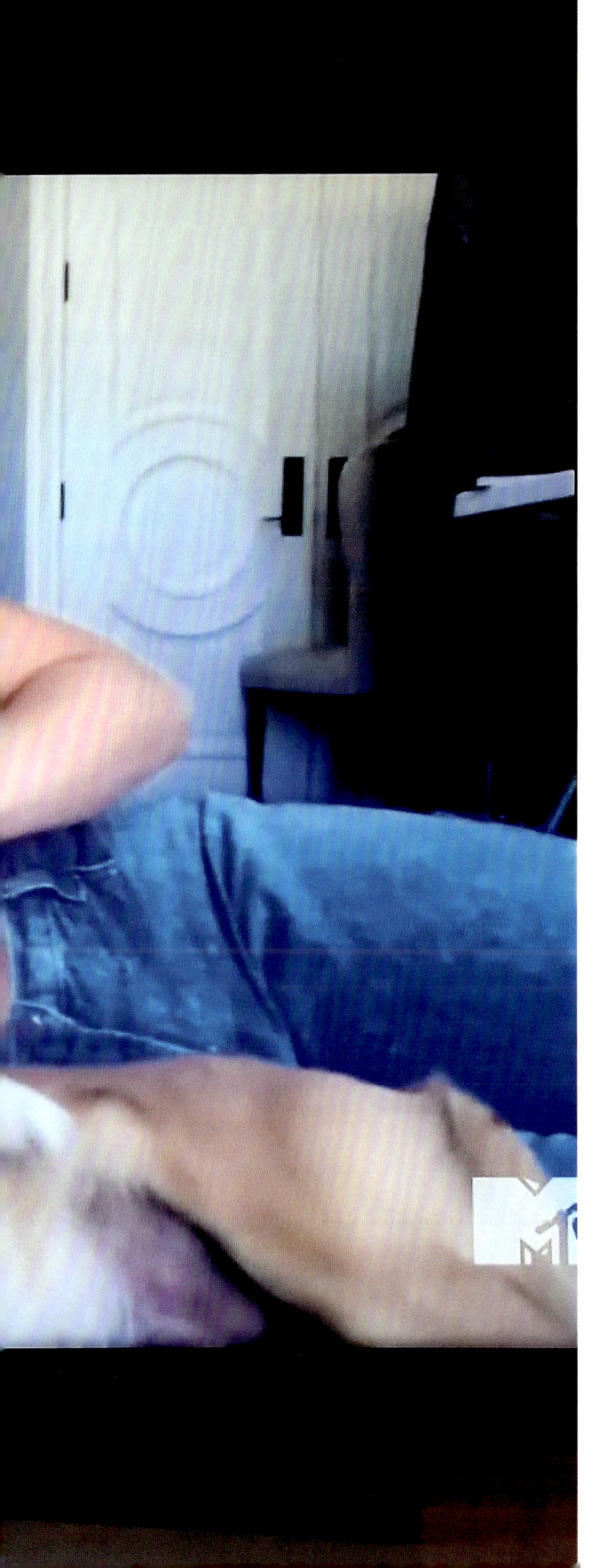

confirmed. She told Sang that the song isn't 100 per cent based on her own lived experiences, but she unquestionably understood the thematic core. 'That fear is something that exists, of course, in your head when you let the trauma part of your brain take the command seat,' she said. 'So I think this was written from that place, and not from a real "I'm in my right mind and I know that I deserve love" place. It was just from the fear place. It deserves to be expressed.' Once she wrote about it, that fear began to dissipate. The Weeknd's verse represented the 'dream reaction' to her anxieties and he 'wrote his verse from a perspective of a person that would be filling certain shoes.'

The singer called 'Off the Table' the centrepiece of *Positions,* telling Sang that it allowed all of the other songs to 'make so much more sense.' The album veered from light-hearted and sexy to complexly emotional as she realized she could be falling in love again.

At the time, *Positions* felt like a clear-cut success, both in terms of Ariana's self-expression and the response from fans. Its songs topped the charts and dominated the radio waves, but behind the scenes, Ariana was less certain. She later confirmed that the response from fans caused her to second-guess some of what she had planned to release around the album and that she 'scrapped so many things.' Speaking on *Las Culturistas* podcast with Bowen Yang and Matt Rogers in 2024, the singer said she felt the release of the LP 'didn't go so well' despite its obvious successes. 'I just got a little bit of, "This is not what we want" vibes,' she recalled. 'I'm very sensitive. But I also understand that as a public figure and a creator, people will either celebrate or tear apart the work. That's part of it. I'm grateful to be here and in acceptance of that.' The discarded releases appear to have included the music video for 'POV', which was shot, but never officially released.

The pandemic was still going strong when Ariana released *Positions*, although the process of developing a vaccine was underway. Like many other artists, Ariana still couldn't tour. She had to find other ways to stay in the forefront of fans' minds. In November 2020, Ariana made a surprise appearance on the televised Adult Swim Festival. Wearing a small pair of her classic cat ears, she teamed up with Thundercat for a rendition of the musician's 2015 track 'Them Changes', which she had previously covered during a BBC Radio 1 Live Lounge session in 2018. The pair were joined by JD Beck and DOMi, and showcased the song in the *Aqua Teen Hunger Force* kitchen. 'It feels like Ariana and I are forever connected through Mac [Miller], and this is part of the healing process,' Thundercat explained of the collaboration. In early December, Mariah Carey released a new remix of her 2010 Christmas song 'Oh Santa!' featuring new vocals from Ariana and Jennifer Hudson. A few weeks later, Ariana delighted fans with the premiere of her concert film *Excuse Me, I Love You*, which debuted on Netflix on 21 December 2020.

Excuse Me, I Love You, directed by Paul Dugdale, was filmed on the Sweetener World Tour in 2019. Most of the footage, both from the stage and behind the scenes, was shot during Ariana's concert at the O2 Arena in London. The film offered a glimpse of Ariana's life on the road while also capturing the dynamic energy of her live show, which was particularly compelling for fans who missed the tour. The singer introduced her tightknit

crew, shared footage of her inner circle – which included Monét – and forced everyone around her to watch her beloved horror movies, including the terrifying *Midsommar*. *Excuse Me, I Love You* wasn't necessarily a revelatory watch, especially for longtime fans, but getting to experience part of Ariana's world for a few hours provided much-needed respite for many viewers. The press agreed. *Entertainment Weekly* wrote of the film, 'Ari did this for her fans not just as an early Christmas present, but an early New Year promise: we'll see each other again soon.'

The new year arrived and touring still seemed like a distant hope. Many countries began offering COVID-19 vaccines to the public – a promise of an eventual return to normality – but it was clear that the world wasn't quite ready for mass gatherings of people, so instead, Ariana continued collaborating. In April 2021, she appeared on a remix of The Weeknd's 'Save Your Tears.' The song landed at No. 1 on the *Billboard* Hot 100, becoming Ariana's sixth top-charting single. The accolade also meant that she and Paul McCartney were the only two artists to achieve three No. 1 duets on the chart. The

remix eventually became Ariana's longest-charting single in the US and galvanized fans, who loved the addition of Ariana's verse and the dual voices on the soaring chorus. The duo performed the song live at the 2021 iHeartRadio Music Awards in May for a masked audience, who shrieked with enthusiasm when Ariana appeared on the stage in a sleek gown. In June, she showed up on Doja Cat's song 'I Don't Do Drugs', which was later nominated for a Grammy. After tapping both artists for *Positions*, it was gratifying for Ariana to return the favour.

Soon, though, Ariana shifted her focus back to the screen. She joined the twenty-first season of the American singing competition *The Voice* as one of the coaches, reportedly becoming the highest-paid coach in the show's history. For this season, which premiered in September, she replaced Nick Jonas to join fellow coaches John Legend, Blake Shelton and Kelly Clarkson. The singer was incredibly excited to be so intimately involved with the talented competitors. 'It's so happy and infectiously joyous,' she said in an interview with *Stage Right Secrets*. 'I also am super moved by how brilliant the performers

'I love everyone so much. I love meeting

PEOPLE

and I felt so invested.'

are and by their voices and the opportunity to work with artists who dream of doing what we get to do is a really fun and cool thing. I feel like I've been doing this for a long time now and maybe I will have some sort of thing to say that will help them execute their dreams.'

The season ran for 26 episodes through December, with one of the groups on Clarkson's team eventually being named the winner. Ariana decided not to return for a subsequent season. She later explained on *Las Culturistas* podcast that she felt too 'emotionally attached' to the contestants. 'That's my problem,' she said. 'I can't really do that because I really get in. I really get in there with everyone. I love everyone so much. I love meeting people, and I felt so invested.' She even stayed in touch with some contestants on social media after the season wrapped. 'I like their posts,' she noted. 'I see their things, I see what they're up to.'

As *The Voice* was airing its final episodes for the season, Ariana began preparing for yet another onscreen coup: *Wicked*. She had quietly been auditioning for the onscreen adaptation of the popular musical for director Jon M Chu and producer Universal Pictures. Her casting as witch Galinda Upland, aka Glinda the Good, opposite Cynthia Erivo as Elphaba Thropp, was announced on 4 November 2021. Chu shared videos of himself telling each actress she had gotten the role. In Ariana's video, she burst into tears. 'I love her so much,' Ariana exclaimed of the character, tears running down her face.

Although the production would not kick off until the following summer, the announcement enlivened Ariana's fans and gave her a boost of momentum as she continued to focus on her acting career.

It was good timing, too. Only a few weeks later, Adam McKay's apocalyptic comedy film *Don't Look Up*, which starred Ariana alongside Leonardo DiCaprio, Jennifer Lawrence, Jonah Hill and Meryl Streep, arrived on Netflix. Ariana played international pop star Riley Bina, a meta appearance that saw the character performing an original song called 'Just Look Up' with Kid Cudi. 'It made sense to have the biggest pop star in the world play the biggest pop star in the world,' McKay explained in a behind-the-scenes feature. 'We got her on set for her first scene with Leo and Jen, and she's improvising lines. I knew she'd nail the song, but I didn't know she could improvise.' According to the director, Ariana added several lines to the final film, including one of his 'favourite moments' in the movie. 'Where you have pretty much the biggest pop star in the world singing beautifully, "We're all gonna die,"' he recalled. 'Every time I see it, it's just this hilarious cognitive dissonance.'

For Ariana, it was delightfully entertaining to 'hold up a mirror' by playing a satirical version of someone like herself. 'I've been a pop star for a long time, so to be able to poke fun at some of the ridiculousness that is so real in this world and what comes with it was really fun and exciting,' she said in the behind-the-scenes feature. Her co-stars also enjoyed the collaboration. Some of them were even real-life fans of the singer. 'I think I was more starstruck to be around Ariana Grande because our worlds don't really collide with the musicians, and what she does is so different,' Lawrence admitted in an interview with *Entertainment Tonight*. 'I've since reflected on my behaviour with Ariana Grande. I went full radio-contest winner.' In interviews, Streep, too, gushed over

'I think
this one
may be your
favorite. It is

MINE.'

working with Ariana, and DiCaprio admitted to *Hits Radio UK*, 'She's fantastic.'

Don't Look Up streamed on Netflix on 24 December 2021, an ideal time for a home release. Reviews were mixed, but critics unequivocally praised Ariana's hilarious performance. *Variety* called her scene performing 'Just Look Up' as the movie's 'funniest gag' while *The Guardian* spotlighted her as a 'good sport' in a less-than-successful film. The reviews didn't deter viewers, nor did they impact the movie's eventual awards success. It earned four Oscar nominations, including Best Picture, and four BAFTA nominations. Ariana's contribution was also noted. The *Critics' Choice* Movie Awards nominated 'Just Look Up' for Best Song, while it won Outstanding Original Song for a Comedy or Musical Visual Media Production at the Society of Composers & Lyricists Awards. Additionally, Ariana, alongside the rest of the cast, was nominated for the Screen Actors Guild Award for Outstanding Performance by a Cast in a Motion Picture.

In 2022, Ariana stepped back out of the public eye. She was preparing to film *Wicked* in the UK and spent months doing extensive vocal training and choreography rehearsals. The film shot over the summer, a career-changing experience for Ariana. Fans waited with anticipation, but first-look images didn't emerge until the following year. It would be many long months before *Wicked* arrived in cinemas and Ariana could discuss her work. Until then, she would have to find ways to fill the time. These included a vocal feature on a new remix of The Weeknd's 2016 song 'Die for You', released on 24 February 2023, and an expanded reissue of her debut album, *Yours Truly (Tenth Anniversary Edition)*. The reissue,

released on 25 August 2023, included live tracks, which were recorded in London. 'I can't wait for you to hear them,' Grande said on Instagram of the new additions. 'This was such a healing and special project to do.'

Once *Wicked* was completed and waiting to be released, Ariana moved on to her next album, *Eternal Sunshine*. The singer had told fans in 2022 not to expect new music until she completed the film, despite rumours to the contrary. But when the SAG-AFTRA strike paused filming in 2023, Ariana headed into the studio and began working on her next album. She soon began to drop hints about it, including posting photos of herself in New York's Jungle City Studios with producer Max Martin and sharing various related images with the caption 'See you next year.' In January 2024, she officially announced *Eternal Sunshine* and shared its debut single 'Yes, And?' alongside a music video that paid homage to Paula Abdul's 1988 video for 'Cold

Hearted'. She described the LP as a 'really vulnerable' concept album, noting in a video on Instagram that it was 'all different heightened pieces of the same story, of the same experience'. She added, to fans, 'I think this one may be your favorite. It is mine'.

'Yes, And?' aptly heralded the album. The upbeat, effervescent pop song was written and produced by Ariana, Max Martin and Ilya Salmanzadeh and boldly addressed the negative press Ariana had been subjected to over the past few years. On the track, she responded to the public conversations about her image, her divorce from Gomez and her new relationship with *Wicked* co-star Ethan Slater, although not all of the lyrics were blatantly obvious. The song suggested that it was better to keep your head up in the face of criticism and simply move forward, never bowing to outside pressure or expectation. It admonished those who tried to own her body or her words, and saw her reclaiming both as her own – an inspirational anthem for anyone who felt unmoored by external and potentially negative forces. The single acknowledged that Ariana had heard all of the gossip about herself and that her response was, 'Yes, and?'

Ariana said she shared the song, and the accompanying video, first because she felt it 'set the tone' for the album by saying 'everyone has shit going on that you don't know about'. She told Zach Sang that the single expressed 'a whole bunch of feelings' that she'd had throughout her career, describing how it responded to the endless dialogue about her body, hair, voice and 'everything'. 'It's like, I'm done. It's done. I'm just going to be', she said.

'I'm just going to be because I fucking love being. I love it, and I want everyone to feel that way as well.'

Ariana felt so passionately about 'Yes, And?' that she released a series of divergent versions of the single after the song debuted at No. 1 on the *Billboard* Top 200 chart. In total, 14 iterations of the track emerged, including an a capella rendition and slowed-down and sped-up mixes. In February, Ariana shared a remix with Mariah Carey, and soon dropped three more remixes with The Blessed Madonna's Godsquad, Jonas Blue and Felix Jaehn. When she announced the version with Carey on Instagram, Ariana described it as 'my one and only, queen of my heart and lifelong inspiration', adding, 'It means more to me than i could ever possibly articulate and i cannot wait for everyone to hear this'. Soon, though, Ariana confirmed that she wouldn't be releasing any further singles from *Eternal Sunshine* before its release. 'As hard as it is to resist the urge to share another song or single with you all asap, I would really love for you to experience the album in full this time', she wrote in an Instagram Story. She added that a complete listen to the LP was her 'ideal way for you all to experience this body of work'.

On 8 March 2024, Ariana released *Eternal Sunshine*, a pop and R&B album that resonated with confidence, both lyrically and musically. Although it embraced Ariana's tried-and-true elements of dance music and synth-pop, it was also a notably introspective collection of songs, reflecting on the singer's personal relationships. Ariana worked with several songwriters and producers, but

WITH THE WEEKND

primarily recorded the album with her trusted collaborator Max Martin. Like its predecessors, *Eternal Sunshine* embraced pop and R&B influences and occasionally incorporated elements of dance music into the tracks. It felt confident, an attribute of many of Ariana's releases. Stepping away to film *Wicked* seemed to have helped her to refocus on what she enjoyed about making music and what she wanted to sing about. It marked a return to singing about romantic relationships, a thematic undercurrent she established in the opening number 'Intro (End of the World)', which saw Ariana asking, 'How can I tell if I'm in the right relationship?'

She explained to Zane Lowe on Apple Music that incorporating the positives and negatives of moving on from a partnership involved a 'tricky balance' during the songwriting process. 'Bye', an upbeat disco-infused track, was the most difficult. 'It was hard for the reason that I desperately didn't want it to sound like a "fuck you", she said on the *Zach Sang Show*, although she didn't specifically say who the song was about. 'I wanted it to sound like, "I need to leave, so bye."' I wanted it to be rooted in self-awareness, and not like, "Fuck you, you go," but 'With love, I'm emigrating from the situation."'

It was easy to assume that *Eternal Sunshine* was about Gomez, who Ariana had married in May 2021 and then filed for divorce in September 2023. The couple kept their marriage relatively private – far more private than Ariana's prior relationships had been, at least – and it was clear from the album's lyrics that the breakup had left scars. 'If you're expecting Sweetener-level optimism from *Eternal Sunshine*, that's not what you're going to get: Grande's latest is a gorgeously exposed journey to the end of her world – or at least what she believes to be the end,' *Rolling Stone* wrote. 'It's a divorce album that goes through all the stages of grief, and the singer navigates a new beginning with some of the most honest and inventive songs of her career so far.' *The Guardian* noted that by releasing the album Ariana reminded listeners that 'love is fallible.' 'Contrary to what some fans might think, the heart does not always deal in moral rectitude,' the review read. 'Putting Grande on a pedestal helps no one, and the beatific, mature *Eternal Sunshine* brings her safely back down to earth.' It seemed important to Ariana that she was never too explicit about her personal life in the songs, allowing the LP to be relatable and perhaps more poetic. *The New York Times* acknowledged this departure from her prior few albums, writing, 'Grande stops short of explicit nods to autobiography and lets swooping, wholehearted emotion tell the story.'

At the same time as the album release, Ariana released a music video for its second single, 'We Can't Be Friends (Wait for Your Love).' Starring actor Evan Peters and directed by Christian Breslauer, the video paid homage to the film *Eternal Sunshine of the Spotless Mind*, starring Jim Carrey as a man attempting to erase the memories of his relationship. 'This video is our own short version of the *Eternal Sunshine* movie, because we felt like that was the perfect thing,' Grande explained in a behind-the-scenes clip. 'Both of the characters end up discontinuing the cycle of their toxic pattern [...] It's kind of about erasing the pain and only wanting the best for someone, even if it means not each other.' The cinematic reference underscored the theme of the dance-ready song: we can move forward, in spite of any discord. It was optimistic, if slightly naive, and a testament to Ariana's sensibility on the album overall.

Instead of simply sending *Eternal Sunshine* out into the world, Ariana released multiple variants, both on CD and vinyl. Two days after the album dropped, she surprised fans with the *Slightly Deluxe* version featuring additional tracks, including 'Supernatural', a collaboration with Troye Sivan. Later that fall, Ariana followed with *Slightly Deluxe and Also Live*, which featured seven live tracks and Brandy and Monica's remix of album cut 'The Boy Is Mine'. That remix, originally released in June 2024, was especially popular. Ariana enlisted the singers after being inspired by their 1998 duet and she even put them in the single's music video, which also starred Penn Badgley. Ariana told Jimmy Fallon on *The Tonight Show* that she had been a 'fan' of the *Gossip Girl* actor her entire life. 'It was so amazing to work with him,' she said. 'Super honoured to work with him.'

'The Boy Is Mine' was a hit, particularly after the remix was released, but it also caused a stir when fans assumed it was about Ariana luring her new boyfriend and *Wicked* co-star Ethan Slater away from his wife. In fact, the song was not written about Slater at all. The sultry R&B number was a loosely reworked version of a leaked song titled 'Fantasize', which Ariana wrote for a scrapped TV show. 'It was like a parody of a 90s girl-group vibe,' she explained on the *Zach Sang Show*, describing the original as 'so corny'. After fans responded positively to the illegally leaked music, Ariana decided to incorporate some 'seedlings' of the song into 'The Boy Is Mine'. 'It's kind of like, "Okay, I'll play the bad girl, here's your bad-girl anthem,"' Ariana told Lowe on Apple Music. She had always wanted to reimagine 'The Boy Is Mine', but wondered whether this was a 'very bad idea'. 'But there is a large group of my fans that really do love a bad-girl anthem, and this is an elevated version of that,' she affirmed.

Although Ariana didn't officially tour *Eternal Sunshine*, she did perform several times throughout 2024. On 9 March 2024, she appeared as the musical guest on *Saturday Night Live*, marking her third time on the show. She performed 'We Can't Be Friends (Wait for Your Love)' and 'Imperfect for You', shifting the focus away from 'Yes, And?' to other tracks on the LP. In May, Ariana was the surprise performer at the Met Gala in New York City. During her set, she joined forces with her *Wicked* co-star Cynthia Erivo for a cover duet of Whitney Houston and Mariah Carey's 1998 single 'When You Believe'. Over the summer, Ariana suggested that she might actually play a few concerts between her promotional obligations for *Wicked* and *Wicked: For Good.* 'I think it would be a really lovely idea to be able to trickle in some shows in between the two *Wicked* films,' she said on the podcast *Shut Up Evan*. 'I think there's a version of that that exists. It's definitely for a

'Okay, I'll
PLAY
the bad girl, here's
your bad-girl
anthem.'

multitude of reasons not going to be a tour in the way that I used to tour.'

Despite the speculation, Ariana eventually confirmed that she didn't have plans to tour in 2024 or 2025. By mid-2024, she began to shift her attention back to *Wicked*, setting a clear boundary between the two sides of her career. 'I think my fans know that music and being on stage will always be a part of my life, but I don't see it coming anytime soon,' she told *Variety* in December. 'I think the next few years, hopefully we'll be exploring different forms of art, and I think acting is feeling like home right now.' While *Eternal Sunshine* had been a success, both commercially and critically, Ariana was determined to move forward into a new chapter – one that would bring her full circle with a long-held childhood dream. She had become a pop star through sheer determination and hard work, but now she was ready to be something even more significant: a movie star.

6

Defying
GRAVITY

WICKED, AWARDS *and* LOOKING FORWARDS

Ariana was ten years old when she first saw the Broadway production of *Wicked*. It was a transformative experience that she later said had divided her life into two parts: before *Wicked* and after *Wicked*. Following the show at New York City's Gershwin Theatre, she was invited backstage to meet the cast. Her mom had won the experience at an auction for Broadway Cares/Equity Fights AIDS, much to Ariana's delight. Kristin Chenoweth, the show's original Glinda, brought the young fan into her dressing room and gifted Ariana with a small bottle of shower gel and a wand. Ariana sang a few bars of *Wicked*'s iconic musical number 'Popular' and helped Chenoweth clean up after the Broadway star's dog peed on the sofa. Before she left, in yet another premonition of what was to come, Ariana announced, 'I want to be Glinda.' In 2024, during an appearance on *The Tonight Show*, Ariana recalled the meeting with Chenoweth, saying, 'I really think it was magical.' It seemed inevitable to her that she would one day be part of the story, a continuation of *The Wizard of Oz* stage production in which she'd starred as a child.

Throughout her career, Ariana continued manifesting the role of Galinda Upland, or Glinda the Good Witch. Early on, she knew she was destined to play the character and her interest in the musical never wavered. In 2013, KiddNation asked Ariana which character she wanted to play in *Wicked*. 'Glinda,' she replied without hesitation. 'For sure. I think that Elphaba's singing part would be more fun,

WITH KRISTIN CHENOWETH

singing-wise. But I'm more of a [Glinda]'. That same year she joined singer-songwriter Mika on his single 'Popular Song', which sampled 'Popular'. She later performed 'The Wizard and I' as part of NBC's *A Very Wicked Halloween: Celebrating 15 Years on Broadway* in 2018, embodying Elphaba in a vibrant green dress. But Ariana was always waiting for the opportunity to realize her long-held ambition to embody Glinda.

It took many years for Ariana's career and the onscreen version of *Wicked* to finally intersect. The development of a film adaptation of Gregory Maguire's 1995 novel

Wicked: The Life and Times of the Wicked Witch of the West began in the 1990s, before the stage musical even existed. Universal Pictures was interested in making a movie version of the book that humanized *The Wizard of Oz*'s villain, the Wicked Witch of the West, but composer Stephen Schwartz eventually persuaded the studio to adapt it for the stage instead. Schwartz wrote the music and lyrics, while Winnie Holzman wrote the book accompanying the musical and it was produced by Universal Stage Productions alongside Marc Platt, Jon B Platt and David Stone. After an initial run at San Francisco's

'I have
never wanted
something as
BADLY
as I did this.'

JOEL GREY AND KRISTIN CHENOWETH ON THE OPENING NIGHT OF *WICKED* ON BROADWAY IN OCTOBER 2003

Curran Theatre, *Wicked* opened on Broadway on 10 June 2003 with Idina Menzel as Elphaba and Chenoweth as Glinda.

Wicked eventually became one of the longest-running Broadway productions to date. As fans clamoured for tickets, rumblings of a potential film continued. Adapting such a magical, vibrant story for Hollywood seemed like an obvious move, but nothing materialized. It wasn't until 2012 that Platt confirmed a film was officially going ahead. In 2016, Universal announced it would be released in 2019 with Stephen Daldry directing. But it was still not yet meant to be. The film version was subsequently put on hold several times and Daldry eventually left due to scheduling issues.

In early 2021, Universal announced a new director: Jon M Chu. He and Platt began to hold auditions, an opportunity that Ariana

jumped on immediately. She had been pursuing the role since the film was initially announced and had prepared accordingly. 'I heard little murmurs of, "Oh, they might start auditioning people for the movie sometime soon,"' Ariana told *W magazine*. 'That was actually three or four years before my first audition. I remember asking my team to check in every now and then and say, "Hey, is this happening? Because if it is, she will pull the plug on just about anything and begin training and vocal lessons."' Once Ariana's team confirmed the auditions were actually happening, she enlisted acting coach Nancy Banks to help prepare monologues and vocal coach Eric Vetro to work on her musical numbers. The singer worked with them every day for three months. 'The really great ones work their asses off, but she wore me down –

ORIGINAL BROADWAY CAST MEMBERS IDINA MENZEL, JOEL GREY AND KRISTIN CHENOWETH

and I mean that delightfully, of course,' Banks told *The Hollywood Reporter* of Ariana's work ethic and drive.

Ariana auditioned for Chu and Platt five times over a three-month period, always arriving at least 30 minutes early. 'I sort of didn't want to believe that she could do this,' Chu told *Vanity Fair*. 'It seems almost too easy to say, "Oh, Ariana Grande." Every time she came in, she was the most interesting person. You just couldn't take your eyes away.' In her first audition, Ariana sang four songs – 'No One Mourns the Wicked', 'Popular', 'Wizard and I' and 'Defying Gravity' – although it was obvious she was auditioning specifically for Glinda because she showed up dressed in pink. For the next meeting, Chu asked Ariana to strip away her pop-star persona. She obliged, coming to the second audition without any makeup and without her signature ponytail. She would have done anything to prove she was right for the role.

'I have never wanted something as badly as I did this,' she said on the *Zach Sang Show*. Persuading them she could do the role meant deconstructing her public persona. 'I had to completely erase popstar Ari – the person that they know so well – because it's even harder to believe someone as someone else when you're so branded as one thing,' she said. 'I had to go all the way and strip that down.' For her final audition, Ariana did a 'chemistry' read with two potential Elphabas, neither of whom were her eventual co-star Cynthia Erivo. The audition lasted more than three hours. In an interview with Billie Eilish at the Directors Guild of America, she recalled being a 'basket case' by the end. 'It was long and thorough, as

it should have been, because these roles, they have to be earned,' she said of the audition process. 'We worked really hard and it was the most gratifying work ever.'

When Chu called her over Zoom in November 2021 to say she'd got the role, Ariana sobbed. 'I love her,' she told the director of Glinda. 'I'm going to take such good care of her.' It was a singular moment for Ariana, who had been waiting for this moment for decades. 'I have never in my life felt the way I did when I found out that I got the role of Glinda in the film,' she told *W*. 'I thought, "Everything's going to be okay forever now."' Erivo sent Ariana a bouquet of pink flowers with a note, which the singer shared on Instagram: 'The part was made for you,' Erivo wrote.

The collaboration between Ariana and her co-star became one of the most essential elements of the film and its eventual promotion. The duo went through their contracts together to ensure they were mutually protected and paid the same amount. They both wanted to start off the project in the most honest way possible. 'There's so much we have in common, but also we're very

different and I never wanted her to feel like there was anything she couldn't share with me or couldn't say to me,' Ariana told *Vanity Fair*'s *Little Gold Men* podcast. 'It was never going to be anything but us against anything that would arise together as a team – us against anything that would come up.'

Ariana flew to London in August of 2022 to begin rehearsals for *Wicked*. Filming was set to start at Sky Studios Elstree in Borehamwood, England, in November, but Chu wanted ample preparation time for the cast. Ariana had already begun transforming her voice before auditioning and she kept working hard after she was cast. 'I've always had a high voice, but it's very different than the register that I use to sing pop music, which is what I was mainly doing,' Ariana explained of her preparation in an interview with Billie Eilish in 2024. 'Just like any other muscles in your body, your vocal cord gets used to what they're trained slowly and surely and taught to do.' She noted that because Glinda lives in a falsetto range it was important for her to spend time working on an operatic, soprano style of singing. 'That's such a pivotal piece of the puzzle when it comes to

Glinda,' she added. The goal was to work on her voice so carefully and thoroughly that once she got to the set she wouldn't have to think about it anymore because her muscles would have developed 'a new memory.' She also pushed herself physically. 'It was phenomenal to see her transform,' the film's cinematographer Alice Brooks told the *Los Angeles Times*. 'Arriving in London for 18 weeks of prep, she had her brown hair and her Ariana Grande look. Week after week, it just slowly changed.'

Despite her successful audition process, Chu recalled thinking that he would need to take a strong hand in guiding Ariana's performance on set. However, he was surprised by the level of preparation she had done, both in terms of her voice and her persona. 'When she showed up on set, she was so Glinda,' Chu told *The Playlist*. 'Whatever she was doing, she was fully immersed. She had done all the readings and all the practice. That's very rare that you get to work with someone in their very first movie leading it, and you get the chance to play.'

The scale of the production for *Wicked* and *Wicked: For Good*, which were shot in tandem and announced as two separate films in 2022, was immense. Massive sets were built on the studio's backlot, including for Shiz University and Emerald City, as well as on location in England. Costume designer Paul Tazewell worked with more than 150 artisans to create the looks for the characters. Glinda's effervescent costumes were inspired by the 1950s, particularly Dior's voluminous silhouette, and the Victorian era, and featured custom embroidery and prints. Everything was lavender and pink, reflecting the good nature of the character. Tazewell worked directly with Ariana and Erivo on each design. 'Their arcs of

'GLINDA'S

makeup made me transform my entire look and my entire relationship to makeup.'

their wardrobes throughout both films were set out before they actually came to start rehearsal,' Tazewell told *ELLE*. 'But then, in those first couple of days, we sat down together with Jon Chu to talk through the designs and what I was planning for each scene to get their way in on how they're starting to see this character.'

Over both films, Tazewell designed around 25 looks for Glinda, including the iconic pink 'bubble' dress she wears as *Wicked* opens, which was inspired by Billie Burke's look in the original 1939 film rather than the stage show. 'Her clothes were so important,' Tazewell told

Harper's Bazaar of Glinda. 'She's this sartorial expert, if you will – a woman who uses femininity and style and elegance to her advantage [...] Many of her looks are based on Hollywood icons.' Glinda's costumes evolved as her character grew emotionally, a journey that Tazewell carefully curated. 'My hope was to create two women [who were] very intentional in how they present themselves,' he told *TODAY*. 'Glinda is privileged. She sees the world through rose-coloured glasses. That's her armour, the same way that Elphaba uses black as her armour. There's nothing accidental about what their styling is. I wanted

for each of them to feel and appear as beautiful as possible, even in how they represent themselves.'

Hair and makeup designer Frances Hannon wanted to emphasize the visual levity and timelessness of Glinda. She drew on style icon of the 1950s and 60s Grace Kelly, to envision Glinda's aesthetic. Each of Glinda's wigs took more than three months to craft and Ariana kept her hair dyed a perfect shade of blonde to keep the hairline seamless. 'We kept her makeup really simple, very accessible,' Hannon told *Gold Derby*. 'We wanted everybody to be able to relate to the characters, very much something that Jon had asked for. And quite iridescent or opalescent so that she had her own reflective quality.' Hannon said she wanted to look for the 'princess' within the character, a sensibility that Ariana herself embraced. 'When Ari would get ready in the morning, the whole process was very much part of Glinda walking onto the set,' Hannon recounted in an interview with *ELLE*. 'We used a lot of her products, R.E.M. Beauty, and there is one highlight called Miss Mercury. At the end of [makeup], she would just put a tiny little dab on the end of her nose. I felt like that was that last little touch that brought her into her space for the day. Then quite often [before a new scene] she'd do it again.'

Ariana described Glinda's look as 'contoured' in a behind-the-scenes video. 'Glinda's makeup made me transform my entire look and my entire relationship to makeup,' Ariana explained. 'I just love it so much.' She particularly loved how Glinda's eyes, with their cat-shaped lashes, weren't heavily lined or creased and that everything was 'warm and open and pretty'. Depending on the costume being worn on a given day, part of Ariana's makeup process was having

her many tattoos covered up. Although Hannon designed Glinda's hair and makeup as part of a specific characterization, she also welcomed Ariana's unique contribution. 'We do it, but they own it,' Hannon said of *Wicked*'s lead cast. 'They add and bring what they want to their character. You can see so much of Ariana Grande, but she absolutely is Glinda.'

On set, it was essential for Ariana, Erivo, and the rest of the actors to actually perform the musical numbers. 'They are the best singers in the world and so every scene they have been singing live,' Chu said in a behind-the-scenes video. 'It was an immediate no-brainer for Cynthia and I,' Ariana added. 'We both were like, "Well, of course we're singing live."' Every scene and musical sequence was performed with live takes on the set. The actors' raw emotion notably came through, particularly in the songs featuring both Ariana and Erivo, such as 'Defying Gravity.' The results were impressive, but it was an immense challenge to shoot. 'Whenever we would get to the end of an incredibly emotional day, Cynthia and I would refer to ourselves as "husks", having given everything we've got,' Ariana reflected in the same behind-the-scenes feature.

Schwartz, the musical's original composer, was involved in reimagining the songs of *Wicked* for the screen. By that point, the musical numbers were deeply familiar to audiences and the filmmakers knew fans would come in with certain expectations of how they would sound. Still, Schwartz wanted to ensure there was a sonic difference between the stage production and the films. The first song Chu shot was 'Popular', a key moment in the story for Glinda and Elphaba. 'In the spirit of being open to new things for the movie, my music team and I thought, "Let's refresh the rhythm,"' Schwartz told the *Los Angeles Times* of the song. '"Let's, maybe, I don't know, hip-hop it up a little bit." Ariana said, "Absolutely not, don't do it. I want to be Glinda, not Ariana Grande playing Glinda."' Ariana later clarified her concerns in an interview with *Variety*, explaining that she first heard the revised track when she arrived in London. 'In the original rehearsal track, they had hip-hop drums,' Ariana said. 'I wanted to lovingly and respectfully say, "Absolutely not!" Thinking through the lens of the character – Galinda Upland does not have that bounce to her at all. She's as vanilla as they come.' She was actually shaking when she called Chu, she said, and asked if they could meet in the middle. 'And of course, it was so understood,' she said. 'And that's what happens when you have a team who loves and respects each other and can hear those truths, because nothing has to be withheld.'

Choreographer Christopher Scott described working with Ariana on the sequence as 'hysterical.' 'You look up and everyone's laughing so hard and Ari's makeup is running down her face because she's been crying laughing,' Scott said to the *Los Angeles Times*. 'I swear it felt like I was working with the modern-day Lucille Ball. And I know we hear a lot, but that's what it felt like. Just how clever and smart she is, and how her comedy is so funny because it's thoughtful.' Although Ariana performed several other musical numbers for *Wicked*, Chu noted that the pressure was most apparent for 'Popular.' 'That's the one everyone's watching and thinking, "All right, Ari, let's see what you got,"' the director told the *Los Angeles Times*. Platt added, 'She was crying after we finished filming it because she was so happy. If you look closely when she's dancing around that hallway, you can really see the genuine joy on her face and it's glorious. Really, it's perfect.'

While in London filming *Wicked,* Ariana removed herself from the rest of her life. She put her music career entirely on pause and focused exclusively on the film. 'In the beginning, I literally had a separate phone,' she told *Vanity Fair*. 'The only numbers were Cynthia and Jon. I was like, "Hi, family? I will speak to you on Sunday."' Healthy boundaries were necessary to protect her mental bandwidth, she explained, noting, 'I can offer myself to this better if something doesn't come in that's like a strange curveball in my head.' She later quipped that her fans noticed how little she was online while in London. 'I wasn't really on social media at all during the filming process,' she told *The Hollywood Reporter*. 'I wasn't really engaged the way that I normally am able to be with them because I just wanted to give myself over fully to this whole experience and not be on my phone that much. They called it "The Dark Ages." I'm not kidding.'

Behind the scenes, a new romance was brewing for Ariana. She and co-star Ethan

'I just wanted to give myself over **FULLY** to this whole experience and not be on my phone that much.'

Slater, who played Boq, began dating in 2023 while the film was still in production. In the months that followed, the tabloids revealed images of the new couple on dates at Disney World, Florida and in New York City, with many speculating that Slater had cheated on his wife to be with Ariana. But the singer smartly refused to play into the online drama. Her divorce from Dalton Gomez was finalized in March of 2024, while Slater completed his divorce from Lilly Jay later that year. In a profile with *Vanity Fair*, Ariana eventually addressed how their relationship was being perceived. 'It definitely doesn't get any easier, seeing some of the negativity that was birthed by disreputable tabloids,' she said. 'Of course, I went through a lot of life changes during the filming of this movie. A lot of people that were working on it did. We were away for two years. So, of course, I understand why it was a field day for the tabloids to sort of create something that paid their bills.' For her, the most disappointing part of the speculation was seeing how many people had believed 'the worst version of it.'

She said that the portrayal of Slater in the media was distorted. 'There couldn't be a less accurate depiction of a human being than the one that the tabloids spread about him,' Ariana noted. 'No one on this earth tries harder or spreads themselves thinner to be there for the people that he loves and cares about. There is no one on this earth with a better heart, and that is something that no bullshit tabloid can rewrite in real life.' Speaking to *GQ*, Slater added, 'There were a lot of big changes in private lives that were really happening, so it's really hard to see people who don't know anything about what's happening commenting on it and speculating, and then getting things wrong about the people you love. So just to address that part of it, that feels really hard.'

Both *Wicked* films were shot together, from the fall of 2022 through the summer of 2023. The production was then forced to pause from 13 July 2023 to 8 November 2023 due to the SAG-AFTRA actors' strike. The actors returned to film the final few scenes in January 2024. Ariana's final day on the *Wicked* set seemed tragically final. 'It was wild,' she said. 'It felt like

a death.' But while the movies themselves were wrapped, there were still months – and even years – of promotion left to do. Audiences caught their first glimpse of the actors as Glinda and Elphaba in April 2023, but the first trailer for *Wicked* didn't arrive until the following year, with a 60-second clip debuting during the Super Bowl in February 2024. Ariana and Erivo joined Chu at the film convention CinemaCon in Las Vegas in April. 'We both felt such a tremendous responsibility to honour these women and to pour our hearts, our souls, our tears – so many different pairs of lashes,' Ariana told the audience as they presented footage from *Wicked*. The official trailer soon followed, as did a summer of marketing and promotion.

In July, Ariana jetted to Paris for the kick-off of the 2024 Summer Olympics. She took the opportunity to promote her R.E.M. Beauty line at Sephora's Champs-Élysées shop, where the singer posed for photos with fans. She re-posted a video from the film's official Instagram account, which showcased the ornate Emerald City train chugging past the Eiffel Tower and across the Seine. She donned an appropriately pink custom Thom Browne gown, which was styled by Mimi Cuttrell, for the opening ceremony, where she delighted in the performances from Lady Gaga and Céline Dion. She was joined by her co-stars Michelle Yeoh and Erivo, who wore a deep-green gown that juxtaposed perfectly with Ariana's look.

'It's a very special moment in our lives, and I'm so thankful I get to share it with Cynthia,' Ariana told *British Vogue* at the event. 'I think my favourite thing about working with Cyn, other than her being such a brilliant and remarkable performer and scene partner, would just be how fully loving, open, and honest we are able to be with each other. I think the thing that made every single day on this set together so beautiful was the space we were able to hold for each other. We laughed, we cried, we learned so much together, from one another and also from these characters we were fortunate enough to play.' Ariana's Audrey Hepburn-inspired gown that she wore at the ceremony hinted at what was to come over the next several months. 'The press tour looks will be simply magical,' Grande teased to *British Vogue*. 'Mimi and I have been having so much fun brainstorming together, we can't wait. Plenty of pink to look forward to, of course! But there are so many gorgeous Oz-ian elements to play off of. We will make Glinda proud.'

It was hard to escape the onslaught of merchandise and product tie-ins that were revealed ahead of *Wicked*. Universal Pictures showcased everything from fashion to games to candles to toys to beauty products, ultimately releasing more than 70 different brand collaborations. Ariana's own R.E.M. Beauty was one of them. She launched a *Wicked*-inspired collection of products, including eyeshadow palettes dubbed 'Ozdust' and skin serum called Galinda Glow Drops. The singer introduced the whimsical collection in a lengthy YouTube video, calling it 'obviously the most exciting drop of the year for us, especially for me [...] I think we really got to bring it to life in a way that will bring the fans even closer,' Ariana said about the translation of the film into products. She added, 'I like it because it doesn't feel like a corny collaboration with a movie. It really feels like everyone cared as much as I do about this film and about these characters and about this world and about honouring Oz in the most loving and respectful way possible.'

'I feel like
I truly came

HOME

to myself in a lot
of ways during
the filming of this
movie...'

The excitement for *Wicked* built more and more as the year went on. It helped that Ariana and Erivo were delightful to watch in their interviews, often speaking side by side. On 21 November 2024, a video of the pair being interviewed by journalist Tracy E Gilchrist went viral. In the clip, Gilchrist said, 'This week, people are taking the lyrics to "Defying Gravity" and really holding space with that.' An emotional Erivo responded, 'I didn't know that was happening. That's really powerful. That's what I wanted.' Ariana gazed at her co-star with genuine recognition and then held one of Erivo's fingers and began to slowly tap it.

The video quickly became a meme that was shared extensively across social media, building anticipation for the film even more. Ariana later explained the meme in an interview with *Variety*, noting, 'I didn't know what any part of it meant.' She said she reached over to Erivo because she 'knew something big was happening' even though she didn't understand exactly what. 'I remember in the moment asking myself, "Am I okay? Did I not hear something?"' Ariana told

Variety. She explained that she grabbed Erivo's finger in solidarity. 'I feel really relieved that the world had the same experience with this moment that I did because I felt like, "Oh, I'm not broken,"' Ariana added. Evan Ross Katz later sent her a T-shirt memorializing the meme.

Wicked arrived in cinemas on 22 November 2024 following several international premieres. A singalong version of the film followed in cinemas in the US on 25 December 2024 and then in other countries. Many fans were surprised to see Ariana's full name, Ariana Grande-Butera, in the credits. But she said it was important to identify herself clearly for something so significant, incorporating both her mom's and her dad's last names. 'I feel like I truly came home to myself in a lot of ways during the filming of this movie, and it was a nice gesture to portray that in the credits by using my full name,' Ariana told *The New York Times* of the decision. 'That was the name of the little girl who saw *Wicked* 20 years ago, and I feel like in a lot of ways I grabbed her hand and said, "Let's go."'

Film critics praised the film, as well as Ariana's performance as Glinda – and particularly her keen ability for humour. 'Grande is supremely well cast,' *The Guardian* wrote. 'It's not just the voice: the singer has a vocal range so extensive that some of it is only audible to bats, and she uses every last note of it here. But more crucial is her gift for physical comedy – each flouncy hair toss, each ditsy heel kick, is a precision-tooled punchline.' The *Los Angeles Times* added, 'Grande is delightful as Galinda, showing off her comedic gifts (honed in the Nickelodeon trenches) and superb voice. She's all big brown eyes and a pout,

which she puts to marvelous use in her performance as the petulant princess of Shiz.'

Audiences, too, were thrilled by the onscreen spectacle. The film was a huge success at the box office and eventually grossed £563 million ($756 million) worldwide. Chenowith, Ariana's longtime hero, was similarly effusive. 'The whole cast is amazing,' the actress said in a video she shared on Instagram after seeing the movie. 'Jon Chu nailed it. I was so moved, emotional, happy, filled with joy.' Even the actor Amanda Seyfried, who also auditioned to play Glinda, acknowledged that Ariana was well cast. 'Everything happens the

way it's meant to,' Seyfried told *People* after the film came out. 'It's an extravaganza, which is what [Ariana] does really well.'

The film's release felt like an essential cultural moment, generating both real conversation and cathartic, emotional singalongs. It encouraged misfits to find community and connection. Ariana and Erivo also emphasized their characters' sexual fluidity and even hinted at deeper feelings between Glinda and Elphaba. 'I think she's a person who loves so much, and I do think that it goes beyond gender, and I think that's a

common theme in Oz,' Ariana explained to *Variety* about Glinda. 'I also think that the ways in which she loves Elphaba so much, and that forgiveness and that unconditional love that they share – I think they're in love with each other. I know, yes, it's platonic.' She added, in an interview with *Gay Times*, 'Whether it's romantic or platonic, Glinda might be a little in the closet, but if there were time you never know. Give it a little more time. But it is just a true love and that transcends sexuality. It's just a deep safety with each other which is probably why people are shipping.'

Ariana said that Glinda lingered with her long after filming. The character's confidence became imbued in her. After waiting so many years to embody Glinda, Ariana was forever changed by the experience. 'There's a part of it that has to do with playing a character that is so sure of herself – even sometimes in a delusional way,' she said. 'It's interesting, because when you slip back into not doing that, your body's like, "Wait a minute. I liked that feeling. I loved believing in myself."' Glinda's voice, too, stayed with Ariana. Because she sang differently to play Glinda, altering her vocals from her usual pop-star range and working on her pronunciation, some fans noticed she sounded perkier than usual. 'I think that might stay,' she told *Variety* of her newly learned speech and singing patterns. 'Galinda required a lot of vocal work

for me. Certain things maybe won't melt away. Some will, but I'm really grateful for the pieces that will stay with us forever. What a beautiful thing to be left with, and to feel the ghost of every day.'

During the *Wicked* press tour, Ariana confronted yet another public controversy. As she appeared on red carpets and in televised interviews, many people – including her fans – began to comment on her weight. The singer and actress had always been small, but some commented that she looked skinnier than usual. During one particular interview, filmed with Erivo in December, Ariana broke down in tears. 'I've been kind of doing this in front of the public and kind of been, you know, a specimen in a petri dish, really, since I was 16 or 17,' Grande said. 'So, I have heard it all. I've heard every version of it, of what's wrong with me. And then you fix it, and

'I'm really

GRATEFUL
for the pieces that
will stay with
us forever.'

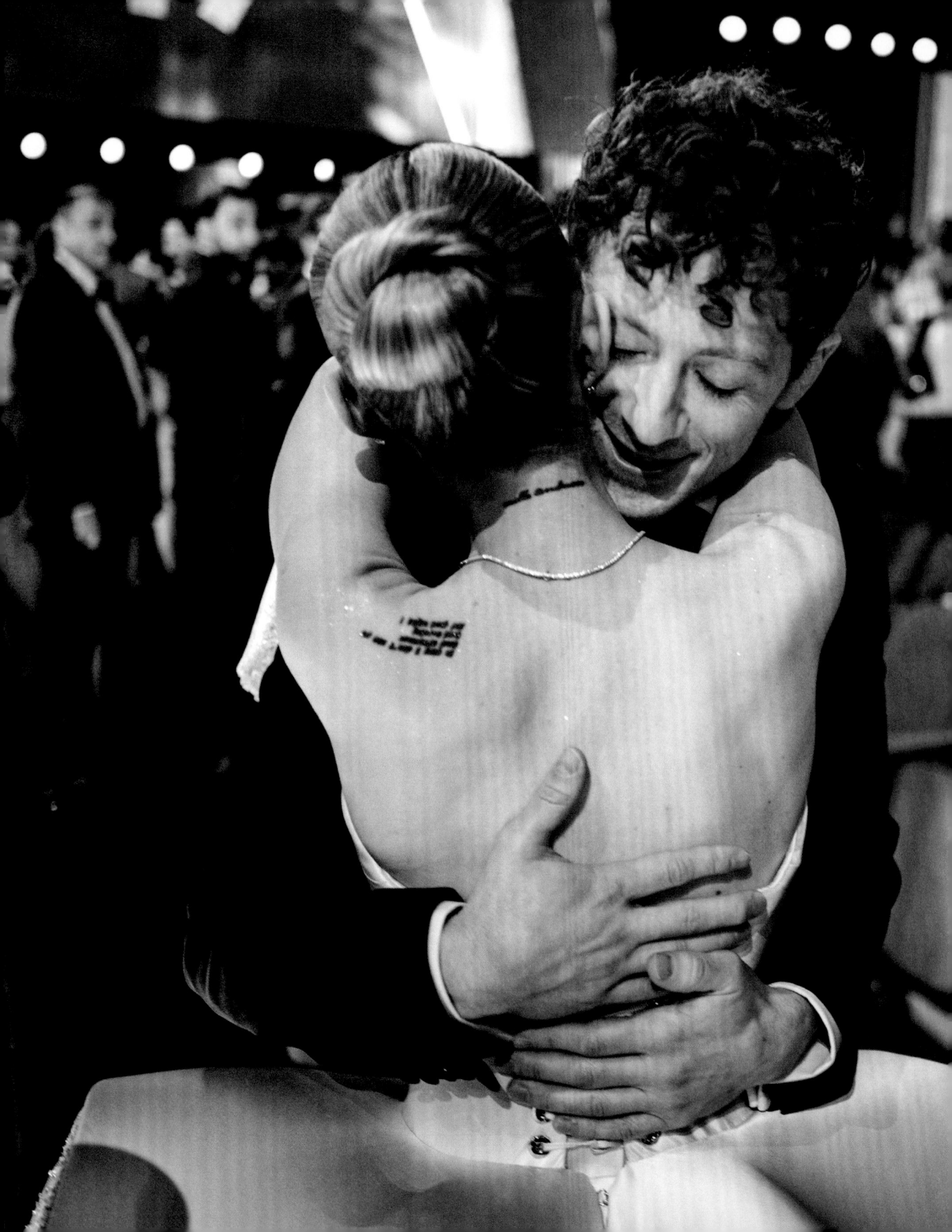

then it's wrong for different reasons.' She acknowledged that it's 'hard to protect yourself from that noise' and that society's obsession with weight and body image is 'dangerous.' 'I'm really lucky to have the support system that I have and to just know and trust that I'm beautiful,' Ariana continued. 'But I do know what the pressure of that noise feels like. It's been a resident in my life since I was 17. I just don't invite it in anymore.'

It wasn't the first time Ariana felt forced to speak up about speculation from fans. In 2023, she released a TikTok video directly addressing people who were body shaming her for her appearance. 'I know personally, for me, the body that you've been comparing my current body to was the unhealthiest version of my body,' Grande shared. 'I was on a lot of antidepressants and drinking on them and eating poorly, and at the lowest point of my life when I looked the way you consider my "healthy". But that, in fact, wasn't my "healthy". She concluded, 'Healthy can look different.' It was clear that, by the time *Wicked* was being promoted, Ariana was exhausted by being forced constantly to explain and defend herself. Her body was no one's business but hers, as many publications and fans affirmed after her December interview with Erivo. Ariana, too, knew what she had to do. 'You all can protect yourselves from that noise – whether it's at a family reunion or online, if you gotta block people, I don't care if you have to delete the app entirely – you keep yourself safe,' she said. 'Because no one has the right to say shit.' Soon, though, the press cycle moved on and shifted back to something more important: was Ariana's performance in *Wicked* awards-worthy?

Although her role in *Wicked* was arguably a starring one, Ariana decided to campaign for the Academy Awards in the Best Supporting Actress category. She explained that she wanted to support Erivo. 'That's how I feel,' she told *Variety*. 'The supporting character, actor, friend, sister to what [she has] done in this film, which is otherworldly.' In the meantime, *Wicked* and its cast and crew began to rack up other accolades and awards. The film became the first fantasy film to win Best Film at the *National Board of Review*, and it was named one of the Top films of 2024 by the American Film Institute. '*Wicked* soars into the stratosphere of cinema history – a modern classic born from an evergreen concoction of cultural landmarks,' the organization shared in a statement. 'The screen has rarely seen – or heard – towering performances like those delivered by Cynthia Erivo and Ariana Grande, leaving audiences Oz-struck across generations.'

In December 2024, *Wicked* was nominated for four awards at the 82nd annual Golden Globe Awards, including Best Motion Picture – Musical or Comedy. Ariana received her first big nomination for Best Supporting Actress – Motion Picture. Speaking to *The Hollywood Reporter* about the nomination, Ariana explained that the recognition felt 'so surreal.' 'We were just very immersed in the work and I was so grateful to have the chance to do the work and I was so excited to do the work every single day,' she said. 'From the lead-up to my first audition to the last day on set on both of the films, I was leading with deep gratitude every day.' She added that she was especially grateful for her fans, who have followed her faithfully through all of the eras of her career. 'It's a beautiful thing to be on this other side of it and for them to recognize the work that I

was doing and to grow with them,' she noted. 'I really have grown up with them my entire career and my entire adult life, and we've been growing alongside each other and they've embraced this new chapter in a way that I'm really deeply grateful for.'

As awards season carried on, *Wicked* continued to be celebrated. The film received 11 nominations at the 30th Critics' Choice Awards and five at the 31st Screen Actors Guild Awards, including for Outstanding Performance by a Cast. By the time the Academy Award nominations were announced in January 2025, it was clear that *Wicked* was an awards juggernaut. The film landed ten nominations, notably Best Actress for Erivo and Best Supporting Actress for Ariana. It felt like the culmination of all her years of hard work to land the role and to bring Glinda to life on screen. 'I sobbed,' she told *Variety* of the moment she heard her name during the announcement. 'I actually haven't stopped sobbing since then. It's been really overwhelming.' Of being nominated alongside Erivo, she added, 'It feels like such a magnificent celebration of this hard work that we were able to do together. It feels like we were passed the wand and broom by Kristin and Idina Menzel. They were nominated for the Tonys together, and now Cynthia and I get to have this recognition together.'

Ariana attended all of the awards shows around the US and jetted overseas to London for the BAFTAs, for which she was also nominated. She embraced glamorous, over-the-top gowns, styled by Cuttrell, and frequently invoked Glinda in her red-carpet looks. She donned a sculptural black and pink Louis Vuitton gown for the BAFTAs, and a whimsical Dior creation at the Critics' Choice

Awards. Not everything was appropriately pink, but Ariana and Cuttrell opted for the hue as often as appropriate. The overall vibe was old Hollywood, just like Glinda's costumes, often relying on classic designers such as Louis Vuitton, Chanel and Givenchy.

For the Academy Awards, Cuttrell ordered two custom Schiaparelli gowns designed by Daniel Roseberry: one to wear onstage during Ariana's opening musical number and one for the high-profile red carpet. To arrive at the awards ceremony, which she attended with her mom, Ariana wore a memorable dusty-pink ensemble that was inspired by Alberto Giacometti lamp and adorned with more than 190,000 crystal sequins, rhinestones and beads. The second gown was ruby red, evoking the iconic shoes from *The Wizard of Oz*. 'I had expressed that I wanted to pay tribute to the ruby slippers and to Judy Garland with this dress, and Daniel really just created the most stunning piece of Ozian art from there,' Ariana told Vogue. 'What a special thing to forever be connected to *Oz*, and to have brought it to life in this way with Daniel.'

The 97th annual Academy Awards, held on 2 March 2025, opened with a tribute to Los Angeles, which had recently been devastated by destructive wildfires across the city. After the applause faded, Ariana appeared on stage, wearing her glittering ruby-red gown, and performed a heartfelt rendition of 'Somewhere Over the Rainbow.' She then yielded the stage to Erivo, who sang a powerful version of Diana Ross's 'Home' from *The Wiz*. Ariana and Erivo then joined forces for a joy-filled performance of *Wicked*'s 'Defying Gravity,' which ended with a rousing standing ovation. 'We wanted it to be a tribute to Oz, and to the beautiful women and witches who have come before us,' Ariana

told *Vogue*. '*The Wizard of Oz*, and especially "Over the Rainbow", has been very special to me since I was a little girl. My grandpa always asked me to sing it, and it has always been a part of my life, becoming even more meaningful to me over the years.'

Although Ariana lost her category to Zoe Saldaña, who was nominated for *Emilia Pérez*, she found the evening to be celebratory and uplifting. After imagining herself as Glinda for so many years, she was being acknowledged for her performance and for her contribution to the film. 'It feels like a dream come true, except it's not even a dream I had ever dreamt,' she admitted to *Vogue*. 'I never even let my mind go that far, to dream that this would ever be a possibility, so it feels just like the most incredible honour. Playing this role was a gift, and was the dream of my life, so this acknowledgement was such an incredible surprise to me, and means so much.' For the singer and actress, having the opportunity to reveal a new side of herself with *Wicked* had been meaningful, so to see it culminate in the Oscars felt miraculous. 'This feeling that people are seeing me – like, actually me – it's so silly because I've been seen for so long,' she told *The Hollywood Reporter*. 'But it feels like it's maybe for the first time and it's just different.'

Fans waited in rapt anticipation for *Wicked*'s sequel, *Wicked: For Good*, to arrive in theatres in the fall of 2025. In the meantime, Ariana released a short film, *Brighter Days Ahead*, as part of a reissue of her 2024 LP *Eternal Sunshine Deluxe: Brighter Days Ahead*. Written and directed by Ariana and Christian Breslauer, the 26-minute film marked her directorial debut and saw her reprising her role from the 'We Can't Be Friends (Wait for Your

Love)' music video. Ariana's father, Edward, in his first acting role, played a mad scientist who created a company called Brighter Days Inc., which Ariana's character Peaches used to relive old memories before they were destroyed. 'This whole short-film concept is basically about how when we're young, sometimes we want to erase certain things or rewrite certain things that seem painful to us in the moment,' Ariana explained in a behind-the-scenes clip. 'But when we grow older, we would do anything to relive those moments and we're so grateful for them and for how they made us who we are and helped us become who we are today.'

After releasing *Brighter Days Ahead* in March, Ariana kept her focus on her acting career. She joined the cast of John Hamburg's fourth instalment in the *Meet the Parents* comedy movie franchise, *Focker In-Law*, alongside original cast members Robert De Niro, Ben Stiller, Teri Polo and Blythe Danner. 'She's going to be really, really funny and kind of the whole engine of the new movie,' Stiller said on *TODAY*. 'So it's exciting.' De Niro added, jokingly, 'The scenes that I have with her will be singing scenes.' She was subsequently cast in an animated film adaptation of the Dr. Seuss children's book *Oh, the Places You'll Go!*, directed by Chu with original songs by composers Benj Pasek and Justin Paul. Ariana's shift to the big screen was intentional. 'I would love to exist in this space for a while longer,' she told *Screen Daily* after *Wicked* came out. 'I love finding characters that make people feel seen and human. I'd love to continue on this road.'

In June, Ariana collaborated with two of her heroes: Barbra Streisand and Mariah Carey. Streisand invited her fellow singers to perform alongside her on 'One Heart, One Voice,' a song on her duets album *The Secret of Life: Partners, Volume Two*. 'When the idea of recording a song with Mariah and Ariana was first suggested, it felt inevitable that it would speak to female empowerment,' Streisand wrote on Instagram. 'The lyrics "We've got every right to make a choice" resonated with me. The song became a vehicle for three strong-willed women to join in voice and purpose.' Ariana couldn't believe the opportunity had finally come her way, calling the song 'a dream come true.' 'Barbra has, quite literally, always been a part of my life,' she said in a behind-the-scenes clip. 'I went to go see Barbra with my mom, and we made it into the concert DVD somehow! We've come a long way from being in the audience to collaborating on the album.' But if fans thought the release would herald more songs from Ariana, they would have to wait. Acting was her priority, although that didn't mean she was done songwriting. In July, Ariana affirmed to fans that she could do both, writing on Instagram that music 'is and has always been my lifeline.' She added, 'there will need to be room made for all of it.'

By the fall of 2025, Ariana and Erivo were back in full swing promoting *Wicked: For Good*. The film's trailer had premiered in the summer, offering a glimpse of Glinda and Elphaba in the latter half of the story. It also teased the duo's highly anticipated duet, 'For Good,' a key moment in the stage production. On

WITH PAMELA ANDERSON

'In the
MOVIE
we get to see her
make the decision
that defines
who she is.'

6 November 2025, NBC aired a live *Wicked* special, featuring Ariana and Erivo, as well as fellow cast members Jeff Goldblum, Bowen Yang, Ethan Slater and Marissa Bode. The singer performed musical numbers from *Wicked* along with a 37-piece orchestra, and took the opportunity to duet with Kristen Chenoweth and Idina Menzel on an uplifting version of 'For Good.' NBC released a live version of the event, *Wicked: One Wonderful Night (Live) – The Soundtrack*, in the lead-up to the film.

Wicked: For Good* arrived in theatres on 21 November 2025. The film featured two original songs, 'The Girl in the Bubble', sung by Grande, and 'No Place Like Home', sung by Erivo. The singers each collaborated with Schwartz on their respective tunes. 'It's a pivotal moment in Glinda's journey,' Ariana explained on *Variety*'s Awards Circuit podcast of this showstopping moment in the sequel. 'It shows a side of her we've never seen before. In the stage show, this transformation happens offstage. But in the movie, we get to see her make the decision that defines who she is. It's a privilege to sing this song and be the first Glinda to bring it to life.'

The film continued Glinda and Elphaba's tumultuous journey and solidified their unbreakable friendship, a core theme of the sequel. Grande said that she related to Glinda's arc as the character discovered her true power. 'I'm sort of working through that as well, the permission to step into your own magic,' she told *The New York Times*. 'It's so funny because in my work, I've always given myself that permission to kindly and lovingly ask for what I need. But when it comes to my real life, that is where I don't know how. It's been a work in progress for years.'

Reviews for the film praised Ariana's performance, noting its comparable depth to the first movie. 'Among the movie's nicer surprises is Grande, who here has the room to turn an irksome caricature into a character,' *The New York Times* wrote, describing Glinda's transformation as one 'that Grande puts across with gestural delicacy and touching vulnerability.' It was easy to understand why Ariana felt so strongly about both the movies and her experience making them. She spoke honestly in interviews about her desire to focus on acting more fully. During an appearance on the *Good Hang with Amy Poehler* podcast, Ariana hinted that she was entering a new chapter, saying 'I think the last 10 or 15 years will look very different to the ones that are coming up.' She added that her 2026 tour might be her last stint on the road for a while. 'I don't want to say any definitive things,' she noted, 'I do know that I'm very excited to do this small tour, but I think it might not happen again for a long, long, long, long time.'

On 21 November 2025, the day *Wicked: For Good* hit cinemas, Ariana officially bid Glinda goodbye. 'thank you, my sweet Glinda, for everything,' she shared alongside a series of photographs of her in costume. 'i will love you always.' But although it was bittersweet to officially leave Glinda and *Wicked* behind her, Ariana optimistically looked forward. There were more acting gigs in her future and more opportunities to showcase her deft talent for onscreen comedy. She would keep singing and keep making music, and she would do it in her own way. After several decades in Hollywood, Ariana understood that there was no right or wrong path as a performer. She wasn't obligated to choose between music and acting simply because the industry expected it. She told *The New York Times* that giving herself so thoroughly to *Wicked* had changed her recent feelings about performing music as a pop star. 'There was something broken about my relationship to pop music that was healed recently through the time away,' she noted. She added, 'I've never felt this connected to my art or inspired, and that's just been such a tremendous gift.'

On the first day of filming *Wicked*, Chu asked Ariana to look into the camera and send a message to her future self. 'I hope you're happy,' she quipped, referencing a line from 'Defying Gravity.' More seriously, Ariana told *Variety*, 'I've never felt this way before, as excited and positively nervous in a good way as I do, ready and sure. And that's something I learned from Glinda.' As she moved on to new films, more music and upcoming tour dates, Ariana would feel that way again – onscreen, in the studio and on the stage.

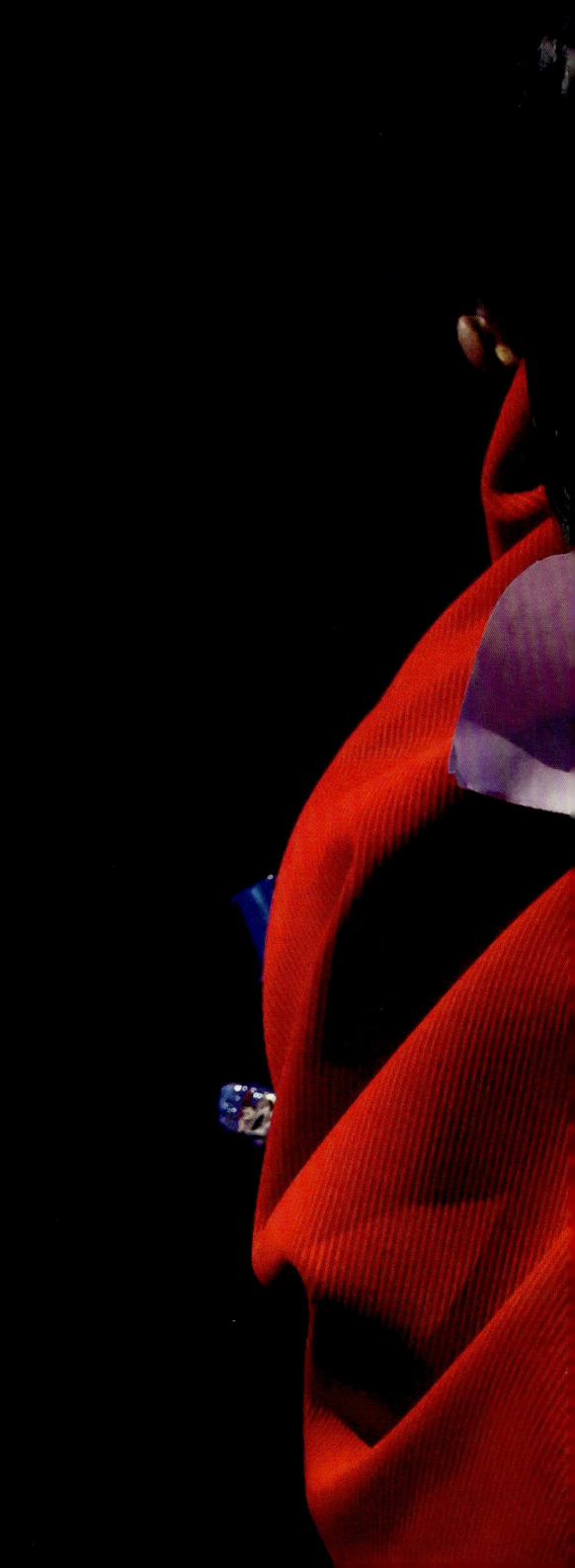

THANK U, NEXT

Since the beginning, Ariana's journey has followed a winding road, with numerous obstacles blocking her path. But she's always surmounted whatever got in her way, even when it seemed nearly impossible. From the outside, it's appeared fairly effortless, as if Ariana knows something about survival that the rest of us haven't learned yet. And because she's been so open about her struggles, often crying publicly and constantly moving through the world with genuine honesty, it's been easy to put her on a pedestal. But Ariana is still the young girl who simply loves to perform. 'The back-and-forth throughout the course of my career has been really hard to navigate mentally,' she told *Vanity Fair* in 2024. 'I was this approachable, funny redhead on Nickelodeon and everyone liked me. And then I had one too many hit records, and everyone decided that I was an evil diva.

And then other terrible things happened, and all of a sudden I was this hero and this victim.'

Being in the spotlight for so many years of her life has meant that Ariana has faced a lot of judgement, often unfairly. As a female celebrity, it's been even worse. There has been an undue obsession with her personal life, particularly her romantic relationships, and the press and public have speculated about her body in a way that is invasive and disrespectful. She has been too sexual and not sexual enough, depending on who you ask. She's been praised for speaking up and told she's oversharing in the same week. But these complexities are what make her so compelling. She's real – and she's not here for any bullshit. It's hard to say how much we really know about Ariana, despite her affinity for directness and honesty. She's called her pop star persona 'a character' and acknowledged that she hasn't always been able to be fully herself under the microscope of fame. 'There are pieces of you and your story that are woven throughout your songwriting, but then, because of the way It travels and becomes sensationalized, it gets away from you,' she told *The Hollywood Reporter* after making *Wicked*. 'And beneath all of it is just a girl from Boca who loves art, and I think that's why it's been such a deeply healing gift to disappear into this character – to take off one mask and put on another.'

What we do know about Ariana without a doubt is her talent. Her sky-high vocals and impressive range easily translate between the stage, recording studio and the big screen. She sings like her life depends on it – and perhaps it does. The comparisons to Mariah Carey have been apt, but Ariana is also her own performer, with her own unique sensibilities and vocal

predilections. She is at home in a variety of musical styles – and *Wicked* proved that her prowess extends far beyond pop music. It's no surprise that Ariana's collaborators and peers have nothing but positive things to say about her and have often complimented her skill. 'I love her,' Mariah Carey told *People* after recording a remix of 'Yes, And?' with the singer in 2024. 'I think she's amazing […] She's super talented, and working together was really fun.' Ariana has always believed in manifesting her future. She believed she would be on television and she was. She believed she would be a performer and she is. But wanting something isn't enough. To achieve these dreams, Ariana worked hard and sacrificed. She missed out on typical teenage experiences to follow her goal of being on stage. Her relationships have been more challenging due to the constraints of her career and being on the road, not to mention the constant speculation from the press. But she has endured because she is an artist and because she has an instinctive need to express herself through that art. She chose this path, but it also chose her. And in her early thirties, she's only scratched the surface of what she can do. 'You can't see one achievement as an indication of anything,' she said on the *Zach Sang Show*. 'You can't accomplish anything and see that as, "I'm different and I can act different and I don't have to work as hard now." It's a complete opposite.' There will be much more in the future from Ariana, whatever she decides to do. She became the pop star she always wanted to be, she fulfilled her longtime dream of embodying Glinda and she embraced both careers simultaneously. She hasn't always been perfect, but Ariana has moved through the challenges in front of her with grace, kindness and a sense of responsibility. She's advocated for women and the LGBTQ+ community, and she resonated with light when the darkness seemed overwhelming after the attack in Manchester. She's a beacon for her fans every day, even when they don't see or hear from her, which is a tribute to how much of herself she's given and will continue to give. When talking to *The Hollywood Reporter* about how she knows when she wants to pursue a particular project, she said, 'I just think it's such an important thing to stay connected to that guttural creative thing in my heart and my chest that wants to give itself over to something that screams at me and says, "Oh, that's a really cool challenge".' 'I have a thing, and when it goes off, I know.' For now, she'll keep living, keep loving and keep picking it up, over and over again.

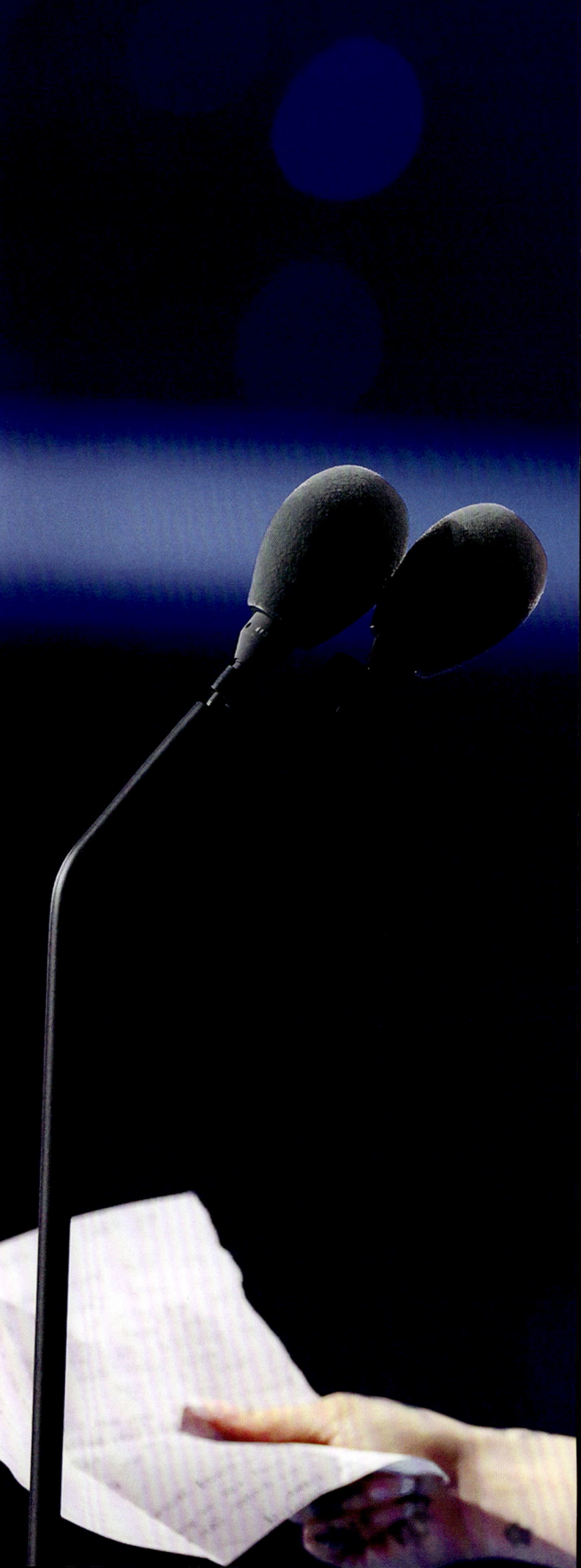

ARIANA GRANDE NOMINATIONS and AWARDS

Ariana Grande has earned numerous accolades and awards throughout her career, including two Grammy Awards. She has frequently been nominated and honoured at the Grammys, for her songs, albums and performances; and over her seven albums, she has received 20 Grammy nominations. She has also frequently received nods at the American Music Awards and the MTV Video Music Awards, as well as at music-awards shows internationally, including the Juno Awards and the Brit Awards. As an actress, Ariana has been nominated for an Academy Award, a Golden Globe Award, a BAFTA Award, three SAG Awards and multiple global critics' awards.

Ariana has always graciously accepted every honour bestowed upon her, often overwhelmed by the wins. When she earned the Grammy for Best Pop Vocal Album for *Sweetener*, she tweeted, 'I know I said I try not to put too much weight into these things....but fuck.......this is wild and beautiful.' Ultimately, though, Ariana has always felt there is something more important than statues. 'I have everything I've ever dreamed of having, and as of late I've discovered that it's the things I've always had and the people I've always had that still make me the happiest,' she said while accepting her Woman of the Year award at *Billboard* Women in Music in 2018.

ALBUMS and EP RELEASES

Yours Truly
30 August 2013

Christmas Kisses EP
13 December 2013

My Everything
22 August 2014

hristmas & Chill EP
18 December 2015

Dangerous Woman
20 May 2016

Sweetener
17 August 2018

Thank U, Next
8 February 2019

Positions
30 October 2020

Eternal Sunshine
8 March 2024

Wicked: The Soundtrack
22 November 2024

Wicked: For Good: The Soundtrack
21 November 2025

GRAMMY AWARDS

BEST POP DUO/GROUP PERFORMANCE, 'Bang Bang' with Jessie J and Nicki Minaj (2015) – *Nominated*

BEST POP VOCAL ALBUM, *My Everything* (2015) – *Nominated*

BEST POP VOCAL ALBUM, *Dangerous Woman* (2017) – *Nominated*

BEST POP SOLO PERFORMANCE, 'Dangerous Woman' (2017) – *Nominated*

BEST POP SOLO PERFORMANCE, 'God Is a Woman' (2019) – *Nominated*

BEST POP VOCAL ALBUM, *Sweetener* (2019) *WON*

ALBUM OF THE YEAR, *Thank U, Next* (2020) – *Nominated*

RECORD OF THE YEAR, '7 Rings' (2020) – *Nominated*

BEST POP SOLO PERFORMANCE, '7 Rings' (2020) – *Nominated*

BEST POP DUO/GROUP PERFORMANCE, 'Boyfriend' with Social House (2020) – *Nominated*

BEST POP VOCAL ALBUM, *Thank U, Next* (2020) – *Nominated*

BEST POP DUO/GROUP PERFORMANCE, 'Rain on Me' with Lady Gaga (2021) *WON*

BEST POP SOLO PERFORMANCE, 'Positions' (2021) – *Nominated*

ALBUM OF THE YEAR, *Planet Her*, Doja Cat with guest turn from Grande (2022) – *Nominated*

BEST POP VOCAL ALBUM, *Positions* (2022) – *Nominated*

BEST POP VOCAL ALBUM, *Eternal Sunshine* (2025) – *Nominated*

BEST POP DUO/GROUP PERFORMANCE, 'The Boy Is Mine' with Brandy and Monica (2025) – *Nominated*

BEST DANCE POP RECORDING, 'Yes, And?' (2025) – *Nominated*

BEST POP DUO/GROUP PERFORMANCE, 'Defying Gravity' with Cynthia Erivo (2026) – *Nominated*

BEST COMPILATION SOUNDTRACK FOR VISUAL MEDIA, *Wicked: The Soundtrack* (2026) – *Nominated*

AMERICAN MUSIC AWARDS

NEW ARTIST OF THE YEAR (2013) – *WON*

FAVORITE POP/ROCK FEMALE ARTIST (2015) – *WON*

ARTIST OF THE YEAR (2015) – *Nominated*

ARTIST OF THE YEAR (2016) – *WON*

FAVORITE SOCIAL ARTIST (2018) – *Nominated*

FAVORITE SOCIAL ARTIST (2019) – *Nominated*

ARTIST OF THE YEAR (2019) – *Nominated*

FAVORITE POP/ROCK FEMALE ARTIST (2019) – *Nominated*

TOUR OF THE YEAR, *Sweetener* World Tour (2019) – *Nominated*

FAVORITE POP/ROCK ALBUM, *Thank U, Next* (2019) – *Nominated*

VIDEO OF THE YEAR, '7 Rings' (2019) – *Nominated*

VIDEO OF THE YEAR, 'Rain on Me' with Lady Gaga (2020) – *Nominated*

COLLABORATION OF THE YEAR, 'Rain on Me' with Lady Gaga (2020) – *Nominated*

FAVORITE SOCIAL ARTIST (2020) – *Nominated*

ARTIST OF THE YEAR (2021) – *Nominated*

FAVORITE POP/ROCK FEMALE ARTIST (2021) – *Nominated*

FAVORITE POP SONG, 'Save Your Tears' with The Weeknd (2021) – *Nominated*

FAVORITE POP/ROCK ALBUM, *Positions* (2021) – *Nominated*

ARTIST OF THE YEAR (2025) – *Nominated*

FAVORITE SOUNDTRACK, *Wicked: The Soundtrack* (2025) – *Nominated*

MTV VIDEO MUSIC AWARDS

BEST FEMALE VIDEO,
'Problem' with Iggy Azalea (2014) – *Nominated*

BEST POP VIDEO, 'Problem' with Iggy Azalea (2014)
– *WON*

BEST LYRIC VIDEO, 'Problem' with Iggy Azalea (2014)
– *Nominated*

BEST COLLABORATION, 'Problem' with Iggy Azalea
(2014) – *Nominated*

BEST COLLABORATION, 'Love Me Harder' with The
Weeknd (2015) – *Nominated*

BEST COLLABORATION, 'Bang Bang' with Jessie J
and Nicki Minaj (2015) – *Nominated*

BEST COLLABORATION, 'Let Me Love You' with Lil
Wayne (2016) – *Nominated*

BEST FEMALE VIDEO, 'Into You' (2016) – *Nominated*

BEST POP VIDEO, 'Into You' (2016) – *Nominated*

BEST EDITING, 'Into You' (2016) – *Nominated*

BEST CINEMATOGRAPHY, 'Into You' (2016)
– *Nominated*

BEST CHOREOGRAPHY, 'Side by Side' with Nicki
Minaj (2017) – *Nominated*

ARTIST OF THE YEAR (2017) – *Nominated*

ARTIST OF THE YEAR (2018) – *Nominated*

VIDEO OF THE YEAR, 'No Tears Left To Cry' (2018)
– *Nominated*

BEST POP, 'No Tears Left To Cry' (2018) – *WON*

BEST CINEMATOGRAPHY, 'No Tears Left To Cry'
(2018) – *Nominated*

BEST VISUAL EFFECTS, 'No Tears Left To Cry' (2018)
– *Nominated*

VIDEO OF THE YEAR, 'Thank U, Next' (2019)
– *Nominated*

SONG OF THE YEAR, 'Thank U, Next' (2019)
– *Nominated*

BEST POP, 'Thank U, Next' (2019) – *Nominated*

BEST DIRECTION, 'Thank U, Next' (2019) – *Nominated*

BEST CINEMATOGRAPHY, 'Thank U, Next' (2019)
– *Nominated*

BEST EDITING, '7 Rings' (2019) – *Nominated*

BEST ART DIRECTION, '7 Rings' (2019) – *WON*

BEST POWER ANTHEM, '7 Rings' (2019) – *Nominated*

SONG OF THE SUMMER, 'Boyfriend' with Social
House (2019) – *WON*

BEST HIP-HOP, 'Rule the World' with 2 Chainz (2019)
– *Nominated*

BEST VISUAL EFFECTS, 'God Is a Woman' (2019)
– *Nominated*

ARTIST OF THE YEAR (2019) – *WON*

VIDEO OF THE YEAR, 'Rain on Me' with Lady Gaga
(2020) – *Nominated*

SONG OF THE YEAR, 'Rain on Me' with Lady Gaga
(2020) – *WON*

BEST POP, 'Rain on Me' with Lady Gaga (2020)
– *Nominated*

BEST CINEMATOGRAPHY, 'Rain on Me' with Lady
Gaga (2020) – *WON*

BEST VISUAL EFFECTS, 'Rain on Me' with Lady Gaga
(2020) – *Nominated*

BEST CHOREOGRAPHY, 'Rain on Me' with Lady
Gaga (2020) – *Nominated*

BEST COLLABORATION, 'Rain on Me' with Lady
Gaga (2020) – *WON*

BEST COLLABORATION, 'Stuck With U' with Justin
Bieber (2020) – *Nominated*

BEST MUSIC VIDEO FROM HOME, 'Stuck With U'
with Justin Bieber (2020) – *WON*

ARTIST OF THE YEAR (2021) – *Nominated*

BEST POP, 'Positions' (2021) – *Nominated*

BEST CHOREOGRAPHY, '34+35' (2021) – *Nominated*

BEST METAVERSE PERFORMANCE, Rift Tour ft. Ariana Grande on Fortnite (2022) – *Nominated*

VIDEO OF THE YEAR, 'We Can't Be Friends (Wait for Your Love)' (2024) – *Nominated*

BEST DIRECTION, 'We Can't Be Friends (Wait for Your Love)' (2024) – *Nominated*

BEST CINEMATOGRAPHY, 'We Can't Be Friends (Wait for Your Love)' (2024) – *WON*

BEST EDITING, 'We Can't Be Friends (Wait for Your Love)' (2024) – *Nominated*

SONG OF THE SUMMER, 'We Can't Be Friends (Wait for Your Love)' (2024) – *Nominated*

ARTIST OF THE YEAR (2024) – *Nominated*

BEST POP ARTIST (2025) – *Nominated*

VIDEO OF THE YEAR, 'Brighter Days Ahead' (2025) – *Nominated*

BEST POP, 'Brighter Days Ahead' (2025) – *Nominated*

BEST LONG FORM VIDEO, 'Brighter Days Ahead' (2025) – *Nominated*

BEST DIRECTION, 'Brighter Days Ahead' (2025) – *Nominated*

BEST CINEMATOGRAPHY, 'Brighter Days Ahead' (2025) – *Nominated*

BEST VISUAL EFFECTS, 'Brighter Days Ahead' (2025) – *Nominated*

BRIT AWARDS

INTERNATIONAL FEMALE SOLO ARTIST (2016) – *Nominated*

INTERNATIONAL FEMALE SOLO ARTIST (2019) – *WON*

INTERNATIONAL FEMALE SOLO ARTIST (2020) – *Nominated*

INTERNATIONAL FEMALE SOLO ARTIST (2021) – *Nominated*

ACADEMY AWARDS

BEST SUPPORTING ACTRESS, *Wicked* (2025) – *Nominated*

BAFTA AWARDS

BEST ACTRESS IN A SUPPORTING ROLE, *Wicked* (2025) – *Nominated*

GOLDEN GLOBE AWARDS

BEST SUPPORTING ACTRESS – Motion Picture, *Wicked* (2025) – *Nominated*

SAG AWARDS

OUTSTANDING PERFORMANCE BY A CAST IN A MOTION PICTURE, *Don't Look Up* (2022) – *Nominated*

OUTSTANDING PERFORMANCE BY A CAST IN A MOTION PICTURE, *Wicked* (2025) – *Nominated*

OUTSTANDING PERFORMANCE BY A FEMALE ACTOR IN A SUPPORTING ROLE, *Wicked* (2025) – *Nominated*

BET AWARDS

BEST NEW ARTIST (2014) – *Nominated*

BET HER AWARD, 'Defying Gravity' with Cynthia Erivo (2025) – *Nominated*

SOURCES

INTRODUCTION

Naomi Pike, 'Miss Vogue Meets: Ariana Grande,' *Miss Vogue*, 29 February 2016

Naomi Pike, 'The World According to Ariana Grande,' *Miss Vogue*, 26 June 2021

Rob Haskell, 'Ariana Grande on Grief and Growing Up,' *Vogue*, 9 July 2019

Srosh Khan and Jasmine Sandhar, 'Ariana Grande Says She's Not Abandoning Music for Film,' *BBC News*, 17 July 2025

Ziya Jaffrey, 'Ariana Grande Was Seemingly Caught Off Guard When a Journalist Told Her That She's the Reason He Met His Partner and Most of His Friends,' *BuzzFeed*, 14 November 2024

ONE: Just Like Magic

'*Billboard* Hot 100,' *Billboard*, 26 June 1993

Broadway.com (@Broadway.com), 'Opening Night: 13,' YouTube, 22 February 2011 <https://www.youtube.com/watch?v=Kqtn48rUChs>

ClevverTV (@ClevverTV), 'Ariana Grande Talks About Her Red Hair,' YouTube, 7 April 2011 <https://www.youtube.com/watch?v=YdmFOwLolJo>

Craig Mclean, 'Ariana Grande: "If You Want To Call Me a Diva I'll Say: Cool"', *The Daily Telegraph*, 17 October 2014

Joe La Puma, 'Ariana Grande: "Shadow of a Doubt"', *Complex*, 5 November 2013

Kim Renfro, 'Why Ariana Grande Always Wears Her Hair Up in That Iconic High Ponytail,' *Business Insider*, 17 July 2018

Leigh Schleps, '"13", The Musical That Kicked Off Ariana Grande's Career, Is Now a Netflix Movie,' *GRAMMY*, 11 August 2022

Lizzy Goodman, 'Ariana Grande on Fame, Freddy Krueger and Her Freaky Past,' *Billboard*, 15 August 2014

Max Gao, 'Elizabeth Gillies on Watching "Quiet on Set" With Ariana Grande Over FaceTime, Reprocessing "Victorious" and How Empowering New Movie "Spread" Tackles the Porn Business,' *Variety*, 16 June 2024

Natalie Weiner, '*Billboard* Woman of the Year Ariana Grande: "There's Not Much I'm Afraid of Anymore"', *Billboard*, 5 December 2018

Podcrushed (@podcrushed), 'Ariana Grande (Part 1) | Podcrushed | Ep 71,' *Podcrushed*, YouTube, 12 June 2024 <https://www.youtube.com/watch?v=AAQGlvnFc1E>

Podcrushed (@podcrushed), 'Ariana Grande (Part 2) | Podcrushed | Ep 72,' *Podcrushed*, YouTube, 17 June 2024 <https://www.youtube.com/watch?v=qW9KbqomKmk>

Rob Haskell, 'Ariana Grande on Grief and Growing Up,' *Vogue*, 9 July 2019

The Hollywood Reporter (@hollywoodreporter), 'Ariana Grande Shares Her Hollywood Firsts: Auditioning for *Wicked*, Being Oscar Nominated & More,' YouTube, 11 February 2025 <https://www.youtube.com/watch?v=AiV-l9aESPAE>

The Kelly Clarkson Show (@kellyclarksonshow), 'Ariana Grande Reflects on Moving to LA for "Victorious"', *The Kelly Clarkson Show*, YouTube, 20 September 2021 <https://www.youtube.com/watch?v=89CPpf4wAZw>

The Tonight Show Starring Jimmy Fallon (@fallontonight), 'Ariana Grande Reacts to Footage from Her First Singing Gig at 8 Years Old,' *The Tonight Show Starring Jimmy Fallon*, YouTube, 5 November 2021 <https://www.youtube.com/watch?v=hJzNWVkW83I>

Will Stroud, 'Frankie Grande Talks Ariana, Gay Acceptance, and the Fight Against AIDS,' *Attitude*, 12 December 2016

Zach Sang (@zachsangshow), 'Ariana Grande | *Eternal Sunshine* Track by Track Breakdown [Part 2],' *Zach Sang Show*, YouTube, 13 March 2024 <https://www.youtube.com/watch?v=dEp1T8GKWaI>

Zach Sang (@zachsangshow), 'Ariana Grande | New Album *Eternal Sunshine*, *Wicked*, Glinda [Part 1],' *Zach Sang Show*, YouTube, 27 February 2024 <https://www.youtube.com/watch?v=zjVU8n_pGzw>

Zach Sang Show Clips (@zachsangshowclips), 'Ariana Grande on Her Hair (High Pony/Cat Valentine Red/Natural Curls),' YouTube, 2 November 2020 <https://www.youtube.com/watch?v=DlH1Ky1sWmA>

TWO: Break Free

Ariana Grande Will Face No Charges Over Doughnut-Licking Incident,' *BBC News*, 14 July 2015

'Ariana Grande's Craziest Diva Demand Yet: She Wants to Be Carried Everywhere!,' *Life & Style*, 10 December 2014

Ariana Grande ft. Zedd. 'Break Free,' *My Everything*, Republic Records, 2014. Written by Anton Zaslavski, Max Martin and Savan Kotecha

Ashleigh Carter, 'Ariana Grande Says "The Way" Feat. Mac Miller Was "The Most Fun" Music Video to Film,' *Teen Vogue*, 26 August 2023

Ashley Lee, 'Ariana Grande Breaks Free and Into Tears at Madison Square Garden: Concert Review,' *The Hollywood Reporter*, 21 March 2015

Brenna Erhlich, 'Ponytail Princess Ariana Grande Wins Best Pop Video VMA,' *MTV News*, 24 August 2014

Brennan Carley, 'Ariana Grande Teases New Album With Big Sean Single,' *SPIN*, 12 August 2014

Brittany Spanos, 'Hear Ariana Grande's Surprise-Released EP "Christmas & Chill"', *Rolling Stone*, 17 December 2015

Bruna Nessif, 'Jennette McCurdy Addresses Ariana Grande Feud: "We Butted Heads at Times but in a Very Sisterly Way"—Watch!,' *E! News*, 10 March 2015

Christina Garibaldi, 'Ariana Grande's "Break Free" the Next Song of the Summer? Zedd Thinks So,' *MTV News*, 30 June 2014

Christopher Rosa, 'Jessie J Wasn't Sure If "Price Tag" Was a Hit or People Were Just "Kissing Her Ass"', *Glamour*, 5 August 2021

Christopher R Weingarten, 'Dangerous Woman,' *Rolling Stone*, 20 May 2016

Corban Goble, '"Problem" [ft. Iggy Azalea],' *Pitchfork*, 13 June 2014

Dan Hyman, 'Life Is Grande: Ariana Grande On Her Debut Album and the Thrill of Hearing Herself on the Radio,' *ELLE*, 22 August 2013

Elisabeth Garber-Paul, 'Jessie J: Why "Bang Bang" Is a Song Young Women Need to Know,' *Rolling Stone*, 8 August 2014

Elyse Dupre, 'Ariana Grande Is So Over "Bang Bang"', *E! News*, 9 October 2018

Emilee Lindner, 'Ariana Grande Is Going Hard for the Honeymoon Tour: Here's Proof,' *MTV News*, 16 January 2015

Emilee Lindner, 'Ariana Grande's "Problem" Has More Than a Few Unexpected Throwbacks,' *MTV News*, 26 April 2014

extratv (@extratv), 'Ariana Grande – "Scream Queens" Set Visit – Full Interview,' YouTube, 6 July 2015 <https://www.youtube.com/watch?v=fAc5wpYUXhE>

Gary Trust, 'John Legend's "All Of Me" Tops Hot 100, Ariana Grande Debuts at No. 3,' *Billboard*, 7 May 2014

Gil Kaufman, 'Ariana Grande Posts Beautiful Message From Her Late Grandpa Before Launching The Honeymoon Tour,' *MTV News*, 25 February 2015

hardknocktv (@hardknocktv), 'Mac Miller talks Album, Ariana Grande, Celebrity Culture,' YouTube, 9 August 2013 <https://www.youtube.com/watch?v=9M4toIUR6Ho>

Jade Biggs, 'Jessie J Apologises to Nicki Minaj Over "Bang Bang" Mixup,' *Cosmopolitan*, 7 August 2021

Jason Lipshutz, 'Ariana Grande Talks "Problem" Single & Second Album, Due Out August/September,' *Billboard*, 28 April 2014

Jason Lipshutz, 'Ariana Grande Talks Breakout Hit "The Way": Watch New Music Video,' *Billboard*, 28 March 2013

Jocelyn Vena, 'Ariana Grande "Working Out a Lot" Before Justin Bieber Tour,' *MTV News*, 29 July 2013

Jocelyn Vena, 'Will Ariana Grande Time-Travel to the '90s for "Baby I" Video?,' *MTV News*, 26 June 2013

Jo La Puma, 'Ariana Grande: "Shadow of Doubt",' *Complex*, 5 November 2013

Jon Caramanica, 'Albums from Neko Case, Ariana Grande, Gorguts and Chelsea Wolfe,' *The New York Times*, 2 September 2013

Julie Naughton, 'Ariana Grande on Fragrances, Fears and Family,' *Women's Wear Daily*, 11 September 2015

Kara K Nesvig, 'Ariana Grande Debunked a Rumor on "Carpool Karaoke" That She Likes to Be Carried Everywhere,' *Teen Vogue*, 16 August 2018

Katie Sharp, 'You've Probably Never Heard of Savan Kotecha, but Everyone Has Heard His Music,' *MIC*, 7 July 2014

Keith Caulfield, 'Ariana Grande's "Problem" Set for Record Sales Debut,' *Billboard*, 5 May 2014

KiddNation (@KiddNationTV), 'Ariana Grande on Kidd Kraddick in the Morning,' YouTube, 26 March 2013 <https://www.youtube.com/watch?v=uxOJ9wb68-o>

Kristin Dos Santos, 'You'll Never Guess How Ariana Grande Was Cast on Scream Queens—and More Scoop from Ryan Murphy!,' *E! News*, 18 September 2015

Kyle Anderson, 'Ariana Grande Teams Up with Iggy Azalea for New Single "Problem"', *Entertainment Weekly*, 28 April 2014

Kyle Buchanan, 'Ariana Grande Doesn't Need a Partner to Feel Complete,' *Cosmopolitan*, 1 March 2017

Madeline Roth, 'Cashmere Cat Debuts New Ariana Grande Song During Honeymoon Tour Kickoff,' *MTV News*, 26 February 2015

Nellie Andreeva, 'Future of Nickelodeon Series "Sam & Cat" in Limbo Amid Behind-the-Scenes Drama,' *Deadline*, 2 April 2014

Nolan Feeney, 'Ariana Grande Is Fully Aware That the Lyrics of "Break Free" Make No Sense,' *TIME*, 7 August 2014

Power 106 Los Angeles (@Power106), 'Ariana Grande Says Why She Wears Cat Ears,' YouTube, 29 September 2014 <https://www.youtube.com/watch?v=8EAzotQ3QZ0>

Recording Academy / GRAMMYs (@RecordingAcademy), 'Ariana Grande Initially Nervous About "Problem"', YouTube, 22 August 2014 <https://www.youtube.com/watch?v=TNpu3z6FEUs>

Rob Sheffield, 'My Everything,' *Rolling Stone*, 26 August 2014

Sal Cinquemani, 'The 21 Best Christmas Albums of the 21st Century,' *Billboard*, 8 December 2015

Shirley Halperin, '*Billboard*'s First Hitmakers Roundtable: 7 of Music's Top Creatives and Influencers on the State of Pop, 10-Second Attention Spans and the Song of the Summer,' *Billboard*, 15 July 2016

Sowmya Krishnamurthy, 'Ariana Grande on "Yours Truly" and Judging Miley Cyrus,' *Rolling Stone*, 11 September 2013

Stephanie Chan, 'Ariana Grande's Honeymoon Tour: See Exclusive Costume Sketches,' *The Hollywood Reporter*, 20 March 2015

Tim Stack, '"Scream Queens" First Look: Ryan Murphy Reveals His New Horror Comedy,' *Entertainment Weekly*, 23 April 2015

Timothy Finn, 'Ariana Grande Delivers a Grand Spectacle at Independence Events Center,' *The Kansas City Star*, 26 February 2015

TMZ (@TMZ), 'Ariana Grande: Tongues New Boyfriend & Donuts!!,' YouTube, 7 July 2015 <https://www.youtube.com/watch?v=Oja-97POVbM8>

Wilfred Chan, 'Ariana Grande Apologizes and Explains Doughnut Licking,' *CNN*, 10 July 2015

THREE: Love Me Harder

Alexandra Topping and Sandra Laville, '"Go Sing With the Angels": Families Pay Tribute to Manchester Victims,' *The Guardian*, 26 May 2017

Alim Kheraj, 'The Surprising Stories Behind Six of Ariana Grande's Biggest Hits,' *Digital Spy*, 16 October 2016

Allison Sadlier, 'Ariana Grande: "Dangerous Woman" U.S. Tour Dates Revealed,' *Entertainment Weekly*, 9 September 2016

Amanda Bell, 'Ariana Grande's "Focus" Is a Lot More Spiritual Than You Think,' *MTV News*, 9 October 2015

Andrea Cheng, 'Ariana Grande Debuts a New Edgy Look for Her Dangerous Woman Tour,' *InStyle*, 6 February 2017

Andrea Dresdale, 'Ariana Grande Opens Up About Manchester Bombing: "It's Still Very Painful"', *Good Morning America*, 18 May 2018

'Ariana Grande Explains Why There Will Be Two "Dangerous Woman" Videos,' *Idolator*, 30 March 2016

Ariana Grande, 'Focus,' Republic Records, 2015. Written by Savan Kotecha, Peter Svensson, Ilya and Ariana Grande

'Ariana Grande Gets Bee Tattoo to Remember Manchester Arena Victims,' *BBC News*, 25 May 2018

'Ariana Grande to Get Honorary Citizenship of Manchester,' *BBC News*, 13 June 2017

'Ariana Grande to Play Manchester Benefit Concert on Sunday,' *BBC News*, 30 May 2017

Bailey Calfee, 'Ariana Grande Promotes Intersectionality With New Feminist Video Interlude,' *Nylon*, 9 March 2019

BBC Radio 1Xtra (@1xtra), 'Ariana Grande Reveals Lil Wayne, Macy Gray and Future Are All on Her New Album,' YouTube, 31 March 2016 <https://www.youtube.com/watch?v=jyvOxukK0OM>

Brennan Carley, 'Ariana Grande Gets Dramatic, Mature, and Whip Smart With Woozy New "Dangerous Woman"', *SPIN*, 10 March 2016

Caryn Ganz, 'Ariana Grande Announces Manchester Benefit Concert, With Special Guests,' *The New York Times*, 30 May 2017

Catherine Thorbecke, 'Ariana Grande on How She Found Healing After Manchester, and How She Knew Pete Davidson Was the One,' *ABC News*, 22 August 2018

Ceylan Yeginsu, Rory Smith and Stephen Castle, 'In Manchester, a Loud Bang, Silence, Then Screaming and Blood,' *The New York Times*, 23 May 2017

Chris Kelly, 'Not Much "Dangerous" About Ariana Grande's Live Performance,' *The Washington Post*, 28 February 2017

Chris Martins, 'Ariana Grande on Defending Female Pop Stars and Staying Away from Drama,' *Billboard*, 19 May 2016

Christopher Rosa, 'The New Ariana Grande Song "Side to Side" Is About Feeling Sore After Hours of Sex,' *Glamour*, 31 August 2016

Dee Lockett, 'With Dangerous Woman, Ariana Grande Shows That Being a Work in Progress Is Serving Her Well,' *Vulture*, 27 May 2016

Elias Leight, 'Ariana Grande Announces US "Dangerous Woman" Tour Dates,' *Rolling Stone*, 9 September 2016

Gary Trust, 'Adele's "Hello" Tops Hot 100 for Second Week; Ariana Grande, Meghan Trainor Hit Top 10,' *Billboard*, 9 November 2015

Giles Hattersley, 'Ariana Grande: The Vogue Interview,' *British Vogue*, 14 August 2018

Greg Evans, 'Barack Obama's Charlottesville Tweet Is Most-Liked Ever; Quotes Nelson Mandela,' *Deadline*, 16 August 2017

Haroon Siddique, 'London Bridge Attacks: How Atrocity Unfolded,' *The Guardian*, 28 June 2017

Helen Pidd, 'Girl Hurt in Manchester Attack Leaves Hospital for Ariana Grande Concert,' *The Guardian*, 4 June 2017

Ian Caramanzana, 'Five thoughts: Ariana Grande at MGM Grand Garden Arena (February 4)', *Las Vegas Weekly*, 6 February 2017

James Hanley, 'Scooter Braun Hails "Unbelievable" Ariana Grande After One Love Manchester Performance', *Music Week*, 6 June 2017

Jon Blisten, 'Ariana Grande Suspends Tour After Manchester Attack', *Rolling Stone*, 23 May 2017

Josh Kurp, 'People Are Only Just Realizing the NSFW Meaning Behind Ariana Grande and Nicki Minaj's "Side to Side"', *UPROXX*, 1 September 2016

Kate Samuelson, 'Queen Elizabeth Responds to "Dreadful" Bombing at Manchester Concert', *TIME*, 23 May 2017

Katie Conner, 'Ariana Grande Is Here to Save Us', *ELLE*, 11 July 2018

Kendall Fisher, 'Ariana Grande Just Changed the Title of Her Upcoming Album and Revealed a Partial Track List', *E! News*, 23 February 2016

Leanna Commins, 'Celebrity Designer Bryan Hearns on Designing for Ariana Grande's Dangerous Woman Tour: Exclusive', *Billboard*, 6 February 2017

Lewis Corner, 'Ariana Grande's New Album Dangerous Woman – Our Track-by-Track First-Listen Review', *Digital Spy*, 18 May 2016

Luis Polanco, 'Ariana Grande Releases "Be Alright" Off "Dangerous Woman"', *Billboard*, 18 March 2016

'Manchester Arena Attack: Bomb "Injured More Than 800"', *BBC News*, 16 May 2018

'Manchester Attack: National Minute's Silence Held', *BBC News*, 25 May 2017

Maria Sherman, 'Ariana Grande Teases "Focus" Single in Debut Perfume Ad', *Fuse*, 20 October 2015

Matthew Strauss, 'Watch Ariana Grande's "Dangerous Woman" Video', *Pitchfork*, 31 March 2016

Meredith B Kile, 'Ariana Grande Announces New Music, Totally Nails Christina Aguilera and Celine Dion Impressions', *ET Online*, 15 September 2015

Mitchell Peters, 'Watch Ariana Grande Debut "Dangerous Woman" Songs on "Saturday Night Live"', *Billboard*, 13 March 2016

Myles Tanzer, 'Ariana Grande', *The Fader*, 30 May 2018

Natalie Weiner, 'Ariana Grande Hints at "Moonlight" Release Date on Twitter', *Billboard*, 3 September 2015

Natalie Weiner, 'Ariana Grande Says "Focus" Doesn't Sound Anything Like the Rest of "Moonlight"', *Billboard*, 6 November 2015

Nerisha Penrose, 'A Timeline of Ariana Grande & Mac Miller's Relationship', *Billboard*, 25 May 2018

'One Love Manchester: Joy Shines Through Pain at Benefit Concert', *BBC News*, 5 June 2017

'Our Favorite Songs Right Now: Kendrick, Ariana Grande and More', *Rolling Stone*, 25 March 2016

Paul Britton, 'Parrs Wood High Schoolgirl Who Stole Nation's Hearts Says Singing With Ariana Was a "Dream Come True"', *Manchester Evening News*, 6 June 2017

'Queen Elizabeth II Visits Victims of the Manchester Arena attack in Hospital', *ABC News*, 25 May 2017

Richard Smirke, 'Scooter Braun On Ariana Grande's "One Love Manchester" Concert: "The City of Manchester Was the Hero"', *Billboard*, 5 June 2017

Rob Haskell, 'Ariana Grande on Grief and Growing Up', *Vogue*, 9 July 2019

Lil Wayne, 'London Roads', FWA, Young Money, 2018. Written by Dwayne Michael Carter, Jr. and London Holmes.

Ryan Reed, 'Hear Ariana Grande's Brash, Brassy New Song "Focus"', *Rolling Stone*, 30 October 2015

Sarah Grant, 'Hear Ariana Grande's Brazen New Track "Into You"', *Rolling Stone*, 7 May 2016

'Scooter Braun: Bringing Light to Darkness', *Big Questions With Cal Fussman*, 29 January 2018

Scooter Braun Projects (@SBProjects), 'One Love Manchester (June 4th 2017)', YouTube, 24 December 2017 <https://www.youtube.com/watch?v=fX9lRv0OtS4>

Sophie Schillaci, 'Ariana Grande Says Her Grandmother Inspired Her Platinum "Focus" Makeover', *ET Online*, 3 November 2015

Tatiana Cirisano, 'Families of Ariana Grande Manchester Concert Bombing Victims Will Each Receive $324,000', *Billboard*, 15 August 2017

The Tonight Show Starring Jimmy Fallon (@fallontonight), 'Ariana Grande Spills All the Tea About Her Album Title and Release', *The Tonight Show Starring Jimmy Fallon*, YouTube, 2 May 2018 <https://www.youtube.com/watch?v=rXqh6AcIb-c>

Zach Johnson, 'Ariana Grande Reunites With Mac Miller in Florida After Manchester Bombing', *E! News*, 23 May 2017

FOUR: The Light Is Coming

Adam White, 'Ariana Grande, O2 Arena, Review: A Night of Magic and Melancholy from the Most Exciting Young Star in Pop', *The Telegraph*, 18 August 2019

Alyssa Bailey, 'All Ariana Grande's Hidden Meanings in Her "Thank U, Next" Album Songs', *ELLE*, 24 January 2019

Alyssa Bailey, 'Ariana Grande's Coachella Performance Had 26 Songs, *NSYNC, Nicki Minaj, Diddy, Mase, and a Mac Miller Tribute', *ELLE*, 15 April 2019

Ana Monroy Yglesias, 'Ariana Grande Shines At Coachella Alongside *NSYNC, Nicki Minaj, Diddy & Mase', *GRAMMY*, 16 April 2019

Andrea Dresdale, 'Ariana Grande Opens Up About Manchester Bombing: "It's still Very Painful"', *Good Morning America*, 18 May 2018

Andrea Park, 'Ariana Grande Asked Madonna to Collaborate Via Text', *W*, 30 October 2018

Anna Iovine, 'Ariana Grande's New Music Video Has a Controversial Ending', *Vice*, 8 February 2019

'Ariana Grande and Justin Bieber Perform Together', *BBC Newsround*, 22 April 2019

'Ariana Grande and Pete Davidson Confirm Engagement', *BBC News*, 21 June 2018

Ben Beaumont-Thomas, 'Coachella Day Three Review: Ariana Grande on Fire and Pusha T on an Iceberg', *The Guardian*, 15 April 2019

Brittany Spanos, 'Review: Ariana Grande Launches *Sweetener* World Tour in Albany, *Rolling Stone*, 19 March 2019

Brittany Spanos, 'Review: Ariana Grande Finds Serenity and Has Some Fun on "Sweetener"', *Rolling Stone*, 20 August 2018

Brittany Spanos, 'Watch Ariana Grande's Cosmic New Video for "God Is a Woman,"' *Rolling Stone*, 13 July 2018

Cady Lang, '"It's Very Sad." Ariana Grande Explains Why She Is Taking a Break from Social Media', *TIME*, 17 October 2018

Christian Allaire, 'Ariana Grande Performed Her New Single During a Surprise Appearance at Coachella', *Vogue*, 21 April 2018

Dan Hyman, 'Mac Miller's Last Days and Life After Death', *Rolling Stone*, 15 November 2018

Elias Leight, 'Some Albums Take Years. Ariana Grande Made "Thank U, Next" In 2 Weeks', *Rolling Stone*, 9 February 2019

Emily Zauzmer, 'Ariana Grande Reflects on Her Major Life Changes: "The Universe Was Like HAAAAAAAAA"', *People*, 8 November 2018

Eric Frankenberg, 'The Sweetener World Tour Finishes as Ariana Grande's Biggest Yet: Final Numbers Are In', *Billboard*, 23 January 2020

Evan Minsker, 'Ariana Grande Details Charlie's Angels Soundtrack', *Pitchfork*, 11 October 2019

Evan Real, 'Frankie Grande on the "Magic" of Watching Sister Ariana Record "No Tears Left to Cry"', *Billboard*, 4 May 2018

Gil Kaufman, 'Ariana Grande Breaks HeadCount Voter Registration Record', *Billboard*, 20 December 2019

Isis Briones, '48 Hours in Hong Kong With Ariana Grande', *Billboard*, 29 September 2017

Jeff Nelson, 'Ariana Grande Claps Back at Tweet Blaming Her for Ex Mac Miller's Relapse, DUI Arrest and Calls Relationship "Toxic"', *People*, 23 May 2018

Jeff Nelson, 'Mac Miller Arrested on Drunk Driving, Hit-and-Run Charges', *People*, 17 May 2018

Joey Nolfi, 'Ariana Grande Shares Breathy Vocals From Dreamy New Song', *Entertainment Weekly*, 1 January 2018

Jon Blistein, 'Hear Ariana Grande Tap Nicki Minaj for Snappy "The Light Is Coming"', *Rolling Stone*, 20 June 2018

Jordan Runtagh, 'Ariana Grande Tells Fans "Life's Too Short to Be Cryptic" About Whirlwind Pete Davidson Romance', *People*, 18 June 2018

Kara K Nesvig, 'Ariana Grande's "God Is a Woman" Was Almost Recorded by Camila Cabello', *Teen Vogue*, 16 December 2019

Katie Connor, 'Ariana Grande Is Here to Save Us', *ELLE*, 11 July 2018

Lars Brandle, 'Ariana Grande Announces "Sweetener" World Tour: See the Dates', *Billboard*, 25 October 2018

Laura Snapes, 'Rapper Mac Miller Dies Aged 26', *The Guardian*, 8 September 2018

Lauren Rearick, 'Ariana Grande Releases "Break Up With Your Girlfriend, I'm Bored" Music Video With Surprise Ending', *Teen Vogue*, 8 February 2019

Lindsay Weinberg, 'Coachella: Ariana Grande's Production Designer on Creating a "Strong, Feminine, Futuristic" World', *The Hollywood Reporter*, 18 April 2019

Madison Bloom and Jazz Monroe, 'Watch Ariana Grande Bring Out Justin Bieber at Coachella 2019', *Pitchfork*, 22 April 2019

Mallory Chin, 'Spotify's 2019 Most-Streamed Artist List', *Hypebeast*, 3 December 2019

Meaghan Garvey, 'No Tears Left to Cry', *Pitchfork*, 20 April 2018

Mickey Boardman, 'In Conversation: Troye Sivan and Ariana Grande', *Paper*, 23 August 2018

Natalie Weiner, '*Billboard* Woman of the Year Ariana Grande', *Billboard*, 5 December 2018

Nerisha Penrose, 'A Timeline of Ariana Grande & Mac Miller's Relationship', *Billboard*, 25 May 2018

'NME's 10 Artists Who Defined the Decade: The 2010s', *NME*, 3 December 2019

Rhian Daly, 'Ariana Grande Shares New Tribute to Mac Miller', *NME*, 14 September 2018

Rhian Daly, 'Ariana Grande's Coachella Headline Set Is a Breathtaking Moment of Light in a Dark World', *NME*, 15 April 2019

Rob Haskell, 'Ariana Grande on Grief and Growing Up', *Vogue*, 9 July 2019

Ryan Reed, 'Hear Ariana Grande's Uplifting New Song "No Tears Left to Cry"', *Rolling Stone*, 20 April 2018

Sam Lansky, 'Ariana Grande Is Ready to Be Happy', *TIME*, 17 May 2018

Sam Sodomsky, 'Ariana Grande Shares Statement on "Toxic" Relationship With Mac Miller', *Pitchfork*, 23 May 2018

Samantha Schnurr, 'See All of Ariana Grande's Sweetener Tour Looks', *E! News*, 19 March 2019

Shad Powers, 'Ariana Grande at Coachella', *Palm Springs Desert Sun*, 21 April 2019

Shanté Honeycutt, 'See How Ariana Grande Managed to Defy Gravity in "No Tears Left to Cry" Video', *Billboard*, 23 April 2018

Shelby Reitman, 'Ariana Grande Makes History as Youngest Coachella Headliner Ever', *Billboard*, 3 January 2019

Steven J Horowitz, 'Ariana Grande's "Sweetener" Producer Breaks Down Its Key Tracks: 'This Is a Career-Defining Album', *Billboard*, 27 August 2018

The Hollywood Reporter and *Billboard* Staff, 'Ariana Grande Takes Over "The Tonight Show" Shares Details on New Album "Sweetener"', *Billboard*, 2 May 2018

Winston Cook-Wilson, 'Ariana Grande – "The Light Is Coming" ft. Nicki Minaj', *SPIN*, 20 June 2018

Xander Zellner, 'Ariana Grande Scores 9th Billboard Hot 100 Top 10 With "No Tears Left to Cry"', *Billboard*, 30 April 2018

Zach Sang (@zachsangshow), 'Ariana Grande "Thank U, Next" Interview', *Zach Sang Show*, YouTube, 9 February 2019 <https://www.youtube.com/watch?v=fpl8v3jiuNU>

Zach Sang (@zachsangshow), 'Ariana Grande Talks God Is a Woman', *Zach Sang Show*, YouTube, 19 August 2018 <https://www.youtube.com/watch?v=qOTPgR9zYUI>

FIVE: Yes, And?

Alyssa Bailey, 'Ariana Grande on Why She Quit Twitter and Chooses Not to Respond to Comments About Her', *ELLE*, 9 July 2024

Alyssa Bailey, 'Watch Ariana Grande and Lady Gaga's Dazzling "Rain on Me" MTV VMAs Performance', *ELLE*, 30 August 2020

Andria Moore, 'Turns Out Ariana Grande Improvised That One Line in "Don't Look Up" — Yes, That One', *Buzzfeed*, 30 December 2021

Anthony D'Alessandro, 'Ariana Grande & Cynthia Erivo To Star in "Wicked" Musical for Universal', *Deadline*, 4 November 2021

Apple Music (@AppleMusic), 'Ariana Grande: "Eternal Sunshine", Wicked & Tour | Apple Music', YouTube, 7 March 2024 <https://www.youtube.com/watch?v=hYAUKSqZ7IE >

Apple Music (@AppleMusic), 'Lady Gaga: Collaborating with Ariana Grande, BLACKPINK and Elton John on "Chromatica" | Apple Music', YouTube, 25 May 2020 <https://www.youtube.com/watch?v=BrmYRxPY95E>

'Ariana Grande Shares How She First Discovered "The Voice"', *Stage Right Secrets*, 16 September 2021

ASCAP (@ascap), 'The Making of "Stuck With U" by Ariana Grande & Justin Bieber', YouTube, 15 June 2020 <https://www.youtube.com/watch?v=ucRB7jpzloE >

Beatrice Verhoeven, '"Encanto," "No Time to Die" and "Don't Look Up" Among Society of Composers and Lyricists Awards Winners', *The Hollywood Reporter*, 8 March 2022

Billboard Staff, 'How Billboard Came to Its Calculations in This Week's Race for the Hot 100 No. 1', *Billboard*, 19 May 2020

Brent Lang, 'SAG Nominations: "House of Gucci" and "Power of the Dog" Score Big; "Succession" and "Ted Lasso" Lead TV', *Variety*, 12 January 2022

Brittany Spanos and Althea Legaspi, 'Ariana Grande Multitasks Running the Country and Home Life in "Positions" Video', *Rolling Stone*, 23 October 2020

Britany Spanos, 'Ariana Grande Is Gorgeously Exposed on "Eternal Sunshine"', *Rolling Stone*, 8 March 2024

Charisma Madarang, 'Ariana Grande Declares "The Boy Is Mine" on "Fallon", Confirms Penn Badgley Will Star in Video', *Rolling Stone*, 7 June 2024

Claire Shaffer, 'Lady Gaga, Ariana Grande Host Cyberpunk Rave in "Rain on Me" Video', *Rolling Stone*, 22 May 2020

Daniel Kreps, 'Ariana Grande Details Week's Worth of "Yours Truly" 10th Anniversary Plans', *Rolling Stone*, 19 August 2023

Daniel Kreps, 'Ariana Grande to Fans Dismissing Coronavirus: "Please Don't Turn a Blind Eye,"' *Rolling Stone*, 15 March 2020

Denise Warner, 'Here Are All the Winners from the 2020 MTV VMAs', *Billboard*, 30 August 2020

Elizabeth Aubrey, 'Ariana Grande Says She Won't Be Releasing Any More Singles Until New Album "Eternal Sunshine" Arrives', *NME*, 5 February 2024

Ellise Shafer, 'Ariana Grande Explains Why She Won't Release an Album During Quarantine', *Variety*, 13 May 2020

'Feud Erupts Over Ariana Grande and Justin Bieber's US Chart Position', *BBC News*, 19 May 2020

Francesca Bacardi, 'Ariana Grande Sending Money to Fans Hit by Coronavirus Shutdowns', *Page Six*, 25 March 2020

Gabe Cohn, 'Grammy Awards 2022: The Full List of Nominees', *The New York Times*, 4 April 2022

Gary Trust, 'Ariana Grande & Justin Bieber's "Stuck With U" debuts at No. 1 on *Billboard* Hot 100', *Billboard*, 18 May 2020

Gary Trust, 'Ariana Grande's "Yes, And?" Debuts at No. 1 on Hot 100', *Billboard*, 22 January 2024

Gary Trust, 'Lady Gaga & Ariana Grande's "Rain On Me" Debuts At No.1 on *Billboard* Hot 100', *Billboard*, 1 June 2020

Gary Trust, 'The Weeknd & Ariana Grande's "Save Your Tears" Soars to No. 1 on *Billboard* Hot 100', *Billboard*, 3 May 2021

Hannah Dailey, 'Ariana Grande Says "We Can't Be Friends" Video Is About "Toxic" Patterns: Watch Behind-the-Scenes Clip', *Billboard*, 13 March 2024

Heran Mamo, 'Ariana Grande Celebrates Hot 100 No. 1 Debut for "Positions," Urges Fans "Pls Vote for Biden"', *Billboard*, 2 November 2020

Joey Nolfi, 'West Side Story, Belfast Storm Oscar Race With 11 Critics Choice Awards Nominations Each: See the Full List', *Entertainment Weekly*, 13 December 2021

Jon Burlingame, '"Don't Look Up's" Musicians on Writing a Song About Impending Doom and Love', *Variety*, 27 January 2022

Jon Lewis, 'Ariana Grande And Justin Bieber Team Up For Fundraising Single "Stuck With U"', *NPR*, 8 May 2020

Karen Mizoguchi, 'Justin Bieber and Ariana Grande Debut "Stuck with U" Video Featuring Celebrity Couples', *People*, 8 May 2020

Karen Mizoguchi, 'Justin Bieber and Ariana Grande to Release New Duet "Stuck with U": "It's Really Good," He Says', *People*, 1 May 2020

Larisha Paul, Ariana Grande Announces Seventh Studio Album "Eternal Sunshine,"' *Rolling Stone*, 17 January 2024

Las Culturistas (@LasCulturistas), 'I've... Been Through' (w/ Ariana Grande) |

Las Culturistas with Matt Rogers and Bowen Yang', YouTube, 6 November 2024 <https://www.youtube.com/watch?v=-kHeeMDzmZM>

Laura Snapes, 'Ariana Grande: Eternal Sunshine Review – Perceptive Post-Divorce Album Is Nearly Spotless', *The Guardian*, 8 March 2024

Lindsay Zoladz, 'Ariana Grande Spins Heartbreak Into Gold on "Eternal Sunshine"', *The New York Times*, 8 March 2024

Lindsay Zoladz, 'On Ariana Grande's "Positions," Intimacy Is a Topic and an Aesthetic', *The New York Times*, 3 November 2020

Liz Calvario, 'Jennifer Lawrence Recalls Fangirling Over Ariana Grande While Filming "Don't Look Up"', *Entertainment Tonight*, 18 November 2021

Madison Bloom, 'Watch Ariana Grande and Thundercat Perform "Them Changes" for Adult Swim Festival', *Pitchfork*, 13 November 2020

Marc Malkin, 'Ariana Grande on Why She Won't Be Touring "Anytime Soon" and How Long She's Known the "Wicked 2" Official Title', *Variety*, 17 December 2024

Mary Sollosi, '7 Things (Other Than Rings) to Love About Ariana Grande Concert Doc Excuse Me, I Love You', *Entertainment Weekly*, 22 December 2020

Matthew Strauss, 'Ariana Grande Says She's Releasing a New Album This Month', *Pitchfork*, 14 October 2020

Nicole Fell, 'Ariana Grande Announces "Eternal Sunshine" Deluxe Album', *The Hollywood Reporter*, 10 March 2025

Peter Debruge, '"Don't Look Up" Review: The Sky Is Falling in Adam McKay's Crank Comet Comedy', *Variety*, 7 December 2021

Raechal Shewfelt, 'Ariana Grande Says She Can't Do The Voice Again Because She Got "So Emotionally Attached" to Contestants', *Entertainment Weekly*, 11 November 2024

Rob Sheffield, 'Review: Ariana Grande Reaches Even Deeper on "Eternal Sunshine Deluxe: Brighter Days Ahead,"' *Rolling Stone*, 28 March 2025

Samantha Hissong, 'Ariana Grande's New Album: Here's Everything We Know', *Rolling Stone*, 23 October 2020

Samantha Vincenty, 'Watch Ariana Grande's SNL Monologue and Sketches from October 12', *NBC*, 13 October 2024

Shirley Halperin and Jem Aswad, 'Rapper 6ix9ine Cries Foul on Ariana Grande, Singer Claps Back as Chart Drama Escalates', *Variety*, 18 May 2020

Skyler Caruso, 'Everything the Star-Studded "Don't Look Up" Cast Has Said About Each Other', *People*, 8 December 2021

StageRightSecrets (@StageRightsSecrets), 'Ariana Grande Interview on Her Biggest "The Voice" Threat', YouTube, 15 September 2021 <https://www.youtube.com/watch?v=bB-vUhDfxtxl>

Tomás Mier, 'Ariana Grande Tears Up as She Describes "Eternal Sunshine" as a "Really Vulnerable" Concept Album', *Rolling Stone*, 1 February 2024

Zach Sang (@zachsangshow), 'Ariana Grande | Eternal Sunshine Track by Track Breakdown [Part 2]', *Zach Sang Show*, YouTube, 13 March 2024 <https://www.youtube.com/watch?v=dEp1T8GKWal>

Zach Sang (@zachsangshow), 'Ariana Grande | New Album Eternal Sunshine, Wicked, Glinda [Part 1]', *Zach Sang Show*, YouTube, 27 February 2024 <https://www.youtube.com/watch?v=zjVU8n_pGzw>

Zach Sang (@zachsangshow), 'Ariana Grande "Positions" Interview', *Zach Sang Show*, YouTube, 31 October 2020 <https://www.youtube.com/watch?v=C0n_aqCcTVk&t=39s>

SIX: Defying Gravity

Advocate Channel (@)AdvocateChannel), 'Wicked's Cynthia Erivo and Ariana Grande on Elphaba and Glinda's Great Platonic Love Story', YouTube, 13 November 2024 <https://www.youtube.com/watch?v=bEsW1KxgtEg>

'AFI Awards 2024 Honorees Announced', *American Film Institute*, 5 December 2024

Aimée Lutkin and Alyssa Bailey, 'Ariana Grande And Ethan Slater's Complete Relationship Timeline', *ELLE*, 24 January 2025

Allyson Payer, 'Ariana Grande Is the It Girl of Award Season—10 of Her Best Looks (So Far)', *Who What Wear*, 20 February 2025

Althea Legaspi, 'Ariana Grande Teases New "Wicked: For Good" Song', *Rolling Stone*, 11 January 2025

Anthony D'Alessandro, 'Ariana Grande & Cynthia Erivo To Star In "Wicked" Musical for Universal', *Deadline*, 4 November 2021

'Ariana Grande Calls for Fans to Stop Body Shaming', *BBC News*, 12 April 2023

'Ariana Grande Has Been Forever Changed by Wicked', *Little Gold Men by Vanity Fair*, Apple, 11 February 2025

Ashley Lee, 'Inside the "Wicked" Musical Number That Could win Ariana Grande an Oscar', *Los Angeles Times*, 25 November 2024

Barbra Streisand ft. Ariana Grande and Mariah Carey. 'One Heart, One Voice', *The Secret of Life: Partners, Volume Two*, Columbia Records, 2025. Written by Jay Landers, William Ross, Charlie Midnight and Walter Afansieff

Beatrice Verhoeven, 'Ariana Grande Reacts to Golden Globes Nomination, Says She's Seen "Wicked" at Least 10 Times', *The Hollywood Reporter*, 9 December 2024

Brett Lang and Jordan Moreau, 'Oscar Nominations 2025: "Emilia Pérez" Leads With 13 Nods, "Wicked" and "The Brutalist" Follow With 10', *Variety*, 23 January 2025

Chris Murphy, 'Wicked Stars Cynthia Erivo and Ariana Grande on Love, Defying Rumors, and Flying High', *Vanity Fair*, 30 September 2024

Chris Willman, 'Billie Eilish Interviews Ariana Grande at "Wicked" Screening, Goes Full Fangirl: "My Brother Used to Be Like: Don't Call Her 'Ari,' You Don't Know Her!"', *Variety*, 5 February 2025

Christian Allaire, 'Ariana Grande Slipped Into Glinda Pink at the 2024 Olympics Opening Ceremony', *British Vogue*, 27 July 2024

Christian Allaire, 'Ariana Grande's 2025 Oscars Fashion Was a "Tribute to Oz"', *Vogue*, 3 March 2025

Clayton Davis and Jordan Moreau, 'SAG Awards 2025 Nominations: "Wicked" and "Shogun" Lead Film and TV With 5 Nods', *Variety*, 8 January 2025

Clayton Davis, 'Critics Choice Awards Nominations: "Conclave" and "Wicked" Lead With 11 Nods Each', *Variety*, 12 December 2024

Daniel D'Addario, 'Ariana Grande and Cynthia Erivo Tell All on "Wicked" Oscar Buzz, Queer Glinda, That Viral Press Tour and What to Expect From Part 2', *Variety*, 2 January 2025

Daniel Montgomery, 'Frances Hannon's "Wicked" Makeup and Hair Magic: From Elphaba's Complexion to Galinda's "Old Hollywood" Glam', *Gold Derby*, 13 February 2025

Dargis Manohla, '"Wicked: For Good" Review: Two Besties Till the End', *The New York Times*, 20 November 2025

David Cote, *Wicked: The Grimmerie: A Behind-the-Scenes Look at the Hit Broadway Musical* (New York City: Hyperion, 2005).

Defying Gravity: The Curtain Rises on Wicked, dir. by Julia Knowles (NBC, 2024).

Eileen Cartter, 'How *Wicked*'s Ethan Slater Made It to Oz and Back', *GQ*, 30 October 2024

Elena Nicolaou, 'What Elphaba's Costume Has to Do With Mushrooms, and More Secrets From the "Wicked" Costume Designer', *Today*, 5 December 2024

Ellie Calnan, 'Ariana Grande on her "Wicked" Journey and Future Acting Projects: "I'd Love To Continue on This Road"', *Screen Daily*, 7 February 2025

'Explore the Behind-the-Scenes Magic of Making Universal Pictures' "Wicked" Movie', *NBCUniversal*, 13 November 2024

Felicia Fitzpatrick, 'Idina Menzel, Kristin Chenoweth, Ariana Grande, and More Celebrate Wicked's 15th Anniversary', *Playbill*, 18 October 2018

Gregory Ellwood, 'Jon M. Chu on The Surprising Cameos That Are More Than Cameos in "Wicked"', *The Playlist*, 25 November 2024

Hannah Dailey, 'Ariana Grande Takes Fans Behind the Scenes of Her "Healing" Short Film for "Brighter Days Ahead"', *Billboard*, 17 April 2025

Hannah Jackson, 'Ariana Grande Transforms Glinda Into a Downtown Girl', *Vogue*, 5 November 2024

Hilary Lewis, '"Wicked" Named Best Film of 2024 by the National Board of Review', *The Hollywood Reporter*, 4 December 2024

Ilana Kaplan, 'Ariana Grande and Ethan Slater Go on Disney Date with Pals: "Her Friends Love Him" (Exclusive Source)', *People*, 26 September 2023

Jamie Sharp, 'Finally – Wicked: The Movie This Way Comes!', *Film Shaft*, 6 September 2011

Jessica Lynch, 'Barbra Streisand Says Collab With Mariah Carey and Ariana Grande "Felt Inevitable"', *Billboard*, 1 July 2025

Jon Burlingame, 'Stephen Schwartz: "Wicked" Movie to Feature "at Least Two" New Songs', *Variety*, 15 May 2017

Justin Kroll, '"Wicked": Jon M. Chu Tapped to Direct Universal's Film Adaptation', *Deadline*, 2 February 2021

Kate McCusker, '"Holding Space": Wicked Has Made the Term Famous. But What Does It Mean?', *The Guardian*, 28 November 2024

Katie Berohn, 'The Beauty Secrets Of "Wicked": How Cynthia Erivo Became Green And Ariana Grande's Holy Grail Product', *ELLE*, 20 November 2024

Katie Walsh, 'Massive "Wicked" Movie Adaptation Takes Its Time to Soar, Much Less Defy Gravity', *Los Angeles Times*, 19 November 2024

KiddNation (@KiddNationTV), 'Ariana Grande on Kidd Kraddick in the Morning', YouTube, 26 March 2013 <https://www.youtube.com/watch?v=uxOJ9wb68-o>

Kyle Buchanan, 'A "Wicked" Tearful Talk With Cynthia Erivo and Ariana Grande', *The New York Times*, 11 November 2024

Lacey Rose, 'The Second Coming of Ariana Grande', *The Hollywood Reporter*, 11 February 2025

Larisha Paul, 'Ariana Grande and Cynthia Erivo Open 2025 Oscars With Powerful "Wicked" Medley', *Rolling Stone*, 2 March 2025

Leigh Scheps, 'Composer Stephen Schwartz Details His Journey Down the Yellow Brick Road', *GRAMMY*, 21 November 2024

Lynn Hirschberg, 'Ariana Grande Has Been Changed for Good', *W*, 3 January 2025

M C Suhocki, 'Ben Stiller Teases Ariana Grande's "Exciting" Role in 4th "Meet the Parents" Film', *Today*, 9 June 2025

Marie-Claire Chappet, 'Creating the World of Wicked With Costume Designer Paul Tazewell', *Harper's Bazaar*, 25 November 2024

Mariel Turner, 'Ariana Grande Tears Up as She Addresses Criticism About Her Appearance: "No One Has the Right to Say S***"', *The Hollywood Reporter*, 6 December 2024

Matthew Belloni, 'Universal Chairman Wants "Fifty Shades" for Summer 2014, More "Bourne" and "Van Helsing" Reboot (Q&A)', *The Hollywood Reporter*, 20 February 2013

Megan Rubenstein, 'Ariana Grande Says Eternal Sunshine Tour Will Be Her "One Last Hurrah"', *E! News*, 18 November 2025

Pamela McClintock, 'Universal's "Wicked" Movie Adaptation Gets December 2019 Release', *The Hollywood Reporter*, 16 June 2016

r.e.m. Beauty (@r.e.m.beauty), 'Ariana Grande Proudly Presents the r.e.m. beauty x Wicked Collection', YouTube, 25 September 2025 <https://www.youtube.com/watch?v=e-zUFjanGNo4 >

Rebecca Rubin, 'Ariana Grande and Cynthia Erivo Light Up CinemaCon With "Wicked" as Director Jon M. Chu Fights Back Tears: "We Dreamed Very Big"', *Variety*, 10 April 2024

Rebecca Rubin, 'Oscar Nomination Reactions: Ariana Grande's Therapist Called to Congratulate Her, Mikey Madison Facetimed Her Dog and Demi Moore Draws Parallels to "Ghost"', *Variety*, 23 January 2025

Sam Damshenas, '"It's True Love2: Wicked's Cynthia Erivo and Ariana Grande on "Gelphie" Ship', *Gay Times*, 22 November 2024

Tamison O'Connor, 'Wicked's Costume Designer On Telling a Timely Story Through Clothes', *ELLE*, 25 November 2024

The Tonight Show Starring Jimmy Fallon (@fallontonight), 'Ariana Grande Talks Eternal Sunshine and Wicked, Teases Penn Badgley Music Video Cameo (Extended)', *The Tonight Show Starring Jimmy Fallon*, YouTube, 7 June 2024 <https://www.youtube.com/watch?v=X-vnJksufEg>

TODAY with Jenna and Friends (@jennaandfriends), 'Kristin Chenoweth Reflects on Meeting a Younger Ariana Grande', *Today With Jenna & Friends*, YouTube, 11 November 2024 <https://www.youtube.com/watch?v=DoJOTLbccgw>

Tommy McArdle and Andrea Mandell, 'Ariana Grande Says She and Cynthia Erivo "Sent Each Other Flowers Immediately" After Golden Globes Nominations (Exclusive)', *People*, 11 December 2024

Toria Sheffield and Nicole Pajer, 'Amanda Seyfried Sets the Record Straight About that Video of Her Singing "Popular" from *Wicked*: "I Was Not Auditioning" (Exclusive)', *People*, 14 December 2024

Variety (@variety), '"Wicked" Stars Ariana Grande & Cynthia Erivo Break Down Viral "Holding Space" Interview', YouTube, 7 December 2024 <https://www.youtube.com/watch?v=a7Inn_IA-MA>

Wendy Ide, 'Wicked Review – Cynthia Erivo and Ariana Grande Make the Magic Happen', *The Guardian*, 24 November 2024

Zach Sang (@zachsangshow), 'Ariana Grande | New Album Eternal Sunshine, Wicked, Glinda [Part 1]', *Zach Sang Show*, YouTube, 27 February 2024 <https://www.youtube.com/watch?v=zjVU8n_pGzw>

Ariana Grande Nominations & Awards

Abid Rahman, '2024 MTV VMAs Nominations: List of Nominees', *The Hollywood Reporter*, 6 August 2024

'All GRAMMY Awards and Nominations for Ariana Grande', *GRAMMY*, 2025

'American Music Awards', *American Music Awards* (NBC, 2025)

'Bafta Film Awards 2025: The Nominations List in Full', *BBC News*, 15 January 2024

Beatrice Verhoeven, 'Ariana Grande Reacts to Golden Globes Nomination, Says She's Seen "Wicked" at Least 10 Times', *The Hollywood Reporter*, 9 December 2024

Brent Lang, 'SAG Nominations: "House of Gucci" and "Power of the Dog" Score Big; "Succession" and "Ted Lasso" Lead TV', *Variety*, 12 January 2022

Brett Lang and Jordan Moreau, 'Oscar Nominations 2025: "Emilia Pérez" Leads With 13 Nods, "Wicked" and "The Brutalist" Follow With 10', *Variety*, 23 January 2025

Clayton Davis and Jordan Moreau, 'SAG Awards 2025 Nominations: "Wicked" and "Shogun" Lead Film and TV With 5 Nods', *Variety*, 8 January 2025

Kyle Buchanan, 'Ariana Grande Still Has Surprises in Store', *The New York Times*, 5 November 2025.

Matt Minton, 'Kendrick Lamar, Doechii and Drake Lead 2025 BET Award Nominations', *Variety*, 8 May 2025

Matthew Strauss, 'MTV VMAs 2025 Nominees Announced: See the Full List Here', *Pitchfork*, 5 August 2025

Olivia Blair, 'Ariana Grande Says 2018 Was "One of the Best and Worst Years of My Life" in *Billboard* Speech', *Cosmopolitan*, 7 December 2018

PICTURE CREDITS

ACKNOWLEDGEMENTS

Writing is a solitary activity, but no book can be achieved alone. Thank you to my agent, Michael Bourret, for support, patience and an endless stream of emails. Thank you to the teams at Dystel, Goderich and Bourret and Abner Stein for such skillful negotiating skills. Thank you to Stephanie Selçuk-Frank, Pauline Bache and everyone at Octopus Publishing Group for bringing me on board and helping to shepherd the book to its release. Thank you to Nikki Dupin and Harriet Smeaton for laying out beautiful pages to accompany my words, and to Jen Veall for diligent photo research.

Most of all, thank you to Ariana Grande and her fans for inspiring me and for creating a community of which I am thrilled to be a part, even in a small way. I hope you enjoy reading this book as much as I enjoyed writing it.

ABOUT THE AUTHOR

Emily Zemler is a writer and journalist based in London. She is a frequent contributor to the *Los Angeles Times* and *Rolling Stone*, among other prestigious outlets. Emily is the author of *The Art and Making of Aladdin*, *Disney Princess: Beyond the Tiara* and *Tim Burton's The Nightmare Before Christmas: Beyond Halloween Town*. She is the co-author of *A Sick Life*, with TLC's Tionne 'T-Boz' Watkins, and *Farewell Yellow Brick Road: Memories of My Life on Tour*, with Elton John.